Southern Rails Around Southampton
Including The Fawley Branch

Ian Drummond

Ian Drummond

For
Stephen Hailes

Holne Publishing

© Holne Publishing & Ian Drummond 2011
British Library Cataloguing in Publication Data
A record for this book is available from the British Library
ISBN 978-0-9563317-2-4
Published by: Holne Publishing, PO Box 343, LEEDS, LS19 9FW
Typesetting and Photo Restoration by: Holne Publishing Services, PO Box 343, LEEDS, LS19 9FW
Printed by: Cambrian Printers Ltd, Llanbadarn Road, Aberystwyth, SY23 3TN

Reasonable efforts have been made to discover the true copyright owners of the photographs reproduced in this volume, and no infringement of copyright is intended. If you have any evidence about the copyright owner of any photograph, or the photographer of any photograph listed as 'photographer unknown', please contact the publisher in the first instance.

Photographs in this volume have been digitally adjusted to enhance clarity, and also remove blemishes, dust etc. However, no intentional alterations have been made to affect their historical significance.

Unless otherwise indicated all maps are based on Ordnance Survey maps of the appropriate date, and their top edge represents north. Maps are reproduced to no particular scale.

Holne Publishing
PO Box 343
LEEDS
LS19 9FW
enquiries@holnepublishing.co.uk
www.holnepublishing.co.uk

Cover Photos:
Front Upper: *Merchant Navy* class Bulleid Pacific locomotive No.35014 *Nederland Line* heads the down *Bournemouth Belle* express, without a headboard, out of Southampton Central on 27th December 1960. In the background is the famous Civic Centre clock tower, and the moon is still in the sky.
Front Lower: *USA* class 0-6-0 tank locomotive No.30073 at Southampton Central station on 10th June 1965. This class of locomotive normally worked in the docks.
(Both Photos: P.F.Bloxam)

Back: The changing face of Southampton's railways as *Berkshire* Diesel Electric Multiple Unit (DEMU) No.1128 stands at Woolston station in the summer of 1966.
(Photo: Terry Hastings)

Contents

Above: On 5th February 1965 No.34098 *Templecombe* departs from Southampton Central with a train bound for York. The Civic Centre clock says that it is 12.05pm, but still the frost can be seen on the sleepers, and steam rises high into the air. No.34098 would last in service until nearly the end of steam, being withdrawn in June 1967. Some will have already observed that the train is departing 'wrong road' because work was going on in the tunnel, which led to single line working being imposed. Note the crane seen where there used to be a connection to the power station across the road. (Photo: P.F.Bloxam)

Foreword

Above: *Merchant Navy* class No.35003 *Royal Mail* waits at Central leaking steam from every orifice, with the up *Pines Express* on 5th January 1965. Ironically this locomotive was the fastest recorded *Merchant Navy* with a speed of 105.88mph. (Photo: P.F.Bloxam)

I am a Sotonian born and bred, and this book's roots go back over thirty-five years to when I was at school. It was then that I wrote a series of unpublished articles on some of Southampton's stations. Even then there was a dream they would make a fascinating book. As part of this a photographic survey of the city's stations was undertaken with my good friend Steve Hailes, to whom this book is dedicated. Sadly many of the photos have now been lost, but some have survived to be included in these pages.

Off and on the idea of a book stayed with me, but then Bert Moody's magnificent *Southampton's Railways* was published, and it seemed that the opportunity was gone. However, now with the changes in technology, and a wealth of new photographic and other material available, it feels as though the time is right for another book on the fascinating history of the railways of this city.

I am indebted to those who have helped with this project. In particular I would like thank Bert Moody, who has given generously of his time to help, and also to Neil Kearns for answering various questions. Special thanks go to Richard Newman and Major Ross Mason, who have contributed sections on life at St Denys station in the 1970s, and the history of Marchwood Military Port, respectively. In addition, I must thank Winston McCanna for his photos of Marchwood Military Port.

So many other photographers have contributed as well, some well known, other less so. All have recorded life on the railways of Southampton over the years, and it is good to recognise their work.

As ever thanks must go to my regular team of helpers Lawrie Bowles, Alan Doe, John and Barbara Plumtree-Varley for their support in dealing with the manuscript. Plus of course my wife, Di, deserves much thanks for encouraging me to make the dream a reality. Thanks go too to the staff at the National Railway Museum, the National Archives at Kew, Hampshire Record Office, and Southampton Record Office.

It is interesting to reflect on how much of what Steve and I set out to observe in the 1970s is now history. Slam-door EMUs, *Hampshire* DEMUs etc. are all now no longer part of the regular railway scene. However, much has been preserved and for this we must be grateful.

One problem has been the wealth of material available, and so there will be a companion book, *Southern Rails on Southampton Docks*, which will look at the development of the dock railways, and other locations. As well as this the line from Redbridge to Romsey via Nursling will appear in a later volume. Regular readers of this series will also note that the size has been increased to A4, primarily to help with the legibility of some of the station plans, but it also enables more photographs to be fitted in as well.

Dreams can come true, but often they take their time.

The Southampton Area Railway Network
Based on Ordnance Survey Map of 1945 with additions

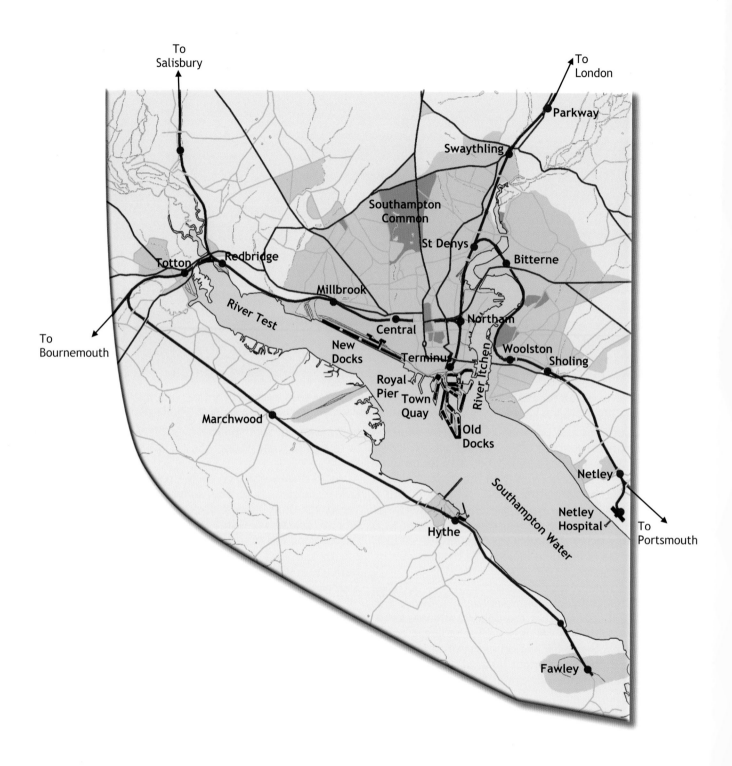

An Overview of Southampton's Early Railway Development

On 6th October 1830 a meeting took place at Bugle Hall, the home of Southampton MP Abel Rous Dottin, that was to change the physical, social and economic landscape of much of south west England. Here it was resolved to form a company to build a railway between Southampton and London that was to become the London and South Western Railway (LSWR).

That the first railway to be built linking London with the south coast was to Southampton might seem obvious today, but in the 1830s it was something of a surprising development. At the time Southampton was a town of some 19,000 inhabitants and poorly regarded as a port. One critic commented that the proposed line would only carry 'parsons and prawns', but all this was to change within a few short years.

Above: The Borough Arms of Southampton.

The Story of Southampton

Geographically Southampton is situated at the confluence of the Rivers Test (to the west) and Itchen (to the east), at the head of a six-mile long, one-mile wide stretch of water known as Southampton Water, which joins the Solent to form an inverted Y with the Isle of Wight at the base. This physical setting contributes to some of Southampton's greatest assets. It is a sheltered port that benefits from a double high tide, with the river waters performing a natural dredging action where they join to form deep channels.

Southampton's history dates back to the Stone Age, and in pre-Roman times there is evidence of trade taking place in the area with the Greeks and Phoenicians. The Romans built a military base at Clausentum near Bitterne Manor on the east shore of the River Itchen. Following their departure in the early 5th century the Saxons established a settlement, around what is now the St Mary's area of the city, called *Hamwic* the origin of the county name of Hampshire.

It was in Medieval times that Southampton developed dramatically, becoming effectively the port for Winchester, and trading with places like Genoa, Spain, Venice and the East. It was also the port from which Henry V embarked for Agincourt. However, it was a later Henry, Henry VIII, who started Southampton's decline with the abolition of the monasteries, which took away much of its trade with Winchester.

However, Southampton continued to operate as a port, and it was from a spot not far from the Royal Pier that the *Mayflower* originally set out for America with those destined to be known as the *Pilgrim Fathers*. But technology was now counting against Southampton, ship sizes were increasing, and Southampton Water was too

sheltered for many of them to navigate easily due to the lack of wind. Therefore, other coastal ports became more significant. Meanwhile during the 18th century Southampton became known as a 'spa' town with people coming to enjoy the bathing. This earned the town the nickname of London-Upon-Mere.

It was not until technology shifted again with the advent of the steamship that Southampton's fortunes were to change once more. Now its sheltered deep water channels were to become an ideal harbour, and in the early nineteenth century the development of modern port and dock facilities began. The railway then became the next logical step in making Southampton a modern port for the age.

The London and Southampton Railway

Following the meeting at Bugle Hall a prospectus was issued for the Southampton, London and Branch Railway and Dock Company on 23rd October 1830. It is worth noting that the original title emphasises that this was a Southampton-driven development, rather than one emanating from the capital as the later title of the London and Southampton Railway Co. (L&SR) would suggest. Very quickly the development of the docks was left to a separate company. A Bill for the railway was submitted to Parliament in the 1833-4 session, the promoters having waited to see the London and Birmingham Railway Bill pass in the previous session before submitting their own plan. On 25th July 1834 the London and Southampton Railway Act received the Royal Assent.

Work started initially with Francis Giles as Engineer, later replaced by Joseph Locke, and funded substantially by industrialists from the north. The first section of the new railway was ready to be opened between Nine Elms, on the south bank of the Thames on the outskirts of London, and Woking Common on 21st May 1838. This was then extended to Winchfield on 24th September 1838, with the

Approximate Routes of Proposed Major Railways

KEY

——————— Railways constructed	·········· Southampton, Petersfield and London Direct Railway
············ Original route of Southampton and Dorchester Railway, proposed Route of Manchester and Southampton Railway	▪▪▪▪▪▪▪▪▪▪▪ Swindon, Southampton and New Forest Railway
▪▪▪▪▪▪▪▪▪▪▪ Shirley Railway	▪▪▪▪▪▪▪▪▪▪▪ Didcot, Newbury and Southampton Junction Railway

Above: An early engraving of the station approach at Southampton station, later Southampton Terminus. Beyond the wall in the background is the dockyard. (Copyright National Railway Museum/SSPL)

section to Basingstoke along with the southern section between Northam in Southampton and Winchester being opened on 10th June 1839. On 11th May 1840 the line was finally completed from Nine Elms to the terminus at Southampton. By this time the Company name had been changed to the LSWR, as a means of gaining favour with the people of Portsmouth for the Company's proposed line from Bishopstoke to Gosport.

Over the years stations opened at Portswood (later named St Denys) in 1861, Northam in 1872, Swaythling in 1883, and, finally for this volume, Southampton Airport in 1966. The original terminal station closed in September 1966 along with the station at Northam.

The Docks

It has already been mentioned that the development of Southampton docks was separated from the railway company in its early days. Therefore, it was left to the Southampton Docks Company, whose Bill received the Royal Assent in May 1836, to commence construction of the facilities. The foundation stone for the first phase was laid on 12th October 1838. By the time of the opening of the Outer Dock on 29th August 1842, a rail connection had already been laid over Canute Road from Southampton station, to allow the direct transfer of cargo from boat to rail and vice versa.

As the docks developed so did its rail network, and in 1892 the LSWR took over the Dock Company to fund future development. Later under the Southern Railway (SR) the New (or Western) Docks were built along the north shore of the River Test, and again rail links were integral to the project.

The Royal Pier and Town Quay

Another waterside rail development was the tramway between Southampton station, the Town Quay, and the Royal Victoria (later simply Royal) Pier. The Town Quay was originally developed in 1803 by the Southampton Harbour Commissioners, who also built the Royal Victoria Pier opened in 1831 by the then Princess Victoria. These remained a separate entity to the docks until 1969.

1845 saw the first proposal for linking Town Quay to Southampton station by means of a tramway, which was eventually opened on 31st December 1847 at a cost of £1,902 9s 5d. The line was leased to the LSWR in 1851 and extended to the Royal Pier in 1871. These lines along with those on the docks will be explored in companion volume *Southern Rails on Southampton Docks*.

The Southampton and Dorchester Railway

A solicitor from Wimborne named Charles Castleman first approached the LSWR board In 1844 with a proposal to build a railway from Southampton to Dorchester. The circuitous route caused it to be nicknamed 'Castleman's Corkscrew', and took an inland route via Ringwood and Wimborne. Bournemouth was avoided because there was little population there at this point, and so it was not considered a great source of traffic.

In the early days of the L&SR it was proposed to build a branch from Basingstoke to Bristol and Bath. This brought it into direct conflict with the Great Western Railway (GWR), and although the line was never built there was continuing friction and competition between the companies for much of the rest of the nineteenth

Above: Mid 19th century engraving showing the Southampton and Dorchester Railway emerging from Southampton tunnel in the distance, through Blechynden station and along the shoreline. Everything to the right of the railway is now re-claimed land.
(Copyright: National Railway Museum/SSPL)

century. In particular the GWR sought on a number of occasions to break the LSWR's monopoly on rail services to and from Southampton, often encouraged by the inhabitants, who felt they would get better service if there was competition. Therefore, over the years the GWR supported many schemes for lines, which in turn meant that the LSWR opposed them, no matter what the potential benefits might have been.

Having struck difficulties with the LSWR, Castleman courted the GWR with the prospect of the railway being built to broad gauge as a means of the GWR gaining access to Southampton. Finally after much negotiation, and Parliamentary intervention, the Bill for the construction of the line received its Royal Assent on 21st July 1845. But by this time the operation of the line had passed to the LSWR and it was to be built to standard gauge.

The original preferred route for the line would have taken it from Redbridge and Millbrook along the shoreline to a terminus at Royal Pier. However, objections from the Harbour Commissioners meant that an alternative route involving following the line of the former Southampton and Salisbury Canal, and then passing through a short tunnel to a junction facing Southampton station at Northam was actually constructed.

On 1st June 1847 the line was opened from a station at Blechynden (later Southampton West from 1858 and Southampton Central in 1935), then on the northern edge of Southampton, to Dorchester. Due to problems with the tunnel, the line was not completely opened until 6th August 1847. Stations were constructed at Redbridge in 1847, Totton in 1859, and, again finally for this volume, Millbrook in 1861. Over the years Blechynden station

grew and developed, particularly following the completion of the Northam Triangle in 1858. This allowed trains from London to directly run onto the Dorchester line, which led to Blechynden, then renamed Southampton West, to become the main station in Southampton, and is now known as Southampton Central.

To Salisbury, Bristol and the North

Between 1845 and 1847 at the height of *Railway Mania* a large number of Bills were submitted to Parliament, which would potentially affect Southampton. Among these were the Oxford, Newbury, Manchester and Southampton Junction Railway, the Southampton, Manchester and Oxford Junction Railway, the Great Manchester, Rugby and Southampton Railway and the Manchester and Southampton Railway (M&SR). While many of these were probably only speculative ventures designed to part investors from their money, the last named line was nearly built.

In 1844 a pamphlet had been circulated advocating a link between Newcastle and Southampton via Oxford. The M&SR was in part a response to this, being sponsored by George Hudson, and Sir John Barker Mill of Mottisfont among others. It was projected to run from a terminus near the Royal Pier via Redbridge, Swindon and Cirencester to link with the Birmingham and Gloucester Railway at Cheltenham, then making use of the Grand Junction Railway between Birmingham and Manchester.

Receiving an enthusiastic response from the people of Southampton, and also having purchased some land, as well as agreement for the railway to pass through the lands of one major landowner, it seemed as if the

Above: Possibly a posed photograph as the locomotive carries no headcode. Drummond designed class C8 4-4-0 No.296 stands at Swaythling station around 1900 with a short train headed by three of the then most modern carriages. These contrast with the 1850s vintage coach body in use as a store on the platform. (Photo: Lens of Sutton Association)

Company's Bill would pass through Parliament. It was therefore something of a surprise when it was thrown out. Most suspicion about its failure fell on the LSWR, who had promoted their own line between Redbridge and Romsey that would have duplicated part of the M&SR's route, but in fact it was also opposed by the GWR who also did not want an independent railway in 'their' territory.

At this point the LSWR opened negotiations with the M&SR for the LSWR to build the line from Redbridge to Andover, and for the M&SR to have running powers over it to Blechynden station. From here the M&SR could build their own line to a terminus by Royal Pier. Sadly this compromise failed to get Parliamentary approval. However, a further joint scheme for part of the line did manage to get through Parliament, but the bursting of the *Railway Mania* bubble meant it was not built.

Meantime the LSWR promoted and built a line from Bishopstoke (Eastleigh) to Milford near Salisbury via Chandler's Ford and Romsey, which opened in 1847. This had the benefit of providing a barrier to unwanted intrusion into Southampton from the north, as well as furthering the Company's ambitions to extend westward towards Exeter and beyond.

This did not prevent further schemes from being put forward for the route and in 1856 the GWR proposed its own broad gauge line from Salisbury to Southampton, but this was rejected. However, in 1858 an independent company, the Andover and Redbridge Railway Co. (A&RR), obtained powers to build a broad gauge railway between the two locations, work starting in 1859, and

even proposed to extend to the Royal Pier. But by means of some subterfuge involving the A&RR's contractor, and after a lengthy Parliamentary battle, the LSWR managed to weaken the A&RR's hand to the point where negotiations between the two started in 1862. This led to the LSWR taking over the A&RR in 1863. Therefore, the line was built to standard gauge, and opened on 6th March 1865, making Redbridge a junction station.

During this time the LSWR had had to deal with another potential rival when in 1861 the Shirley Railway was proposed. This scheme would have run from the Royal Pier across the LSWR just west of Blechynden at Hill Lane, and continued through Upper Shirley, not far from the house where the author was raised. From here it would have traversed Dale Valley and on to a junction with the A&RR at Nursling, a total distance of 2.2 miles. It failed to be authorised, along with another application from the Southampton, Shirley and Nursling Railway in 1863.

However, the main potential invader from the North was yet to come. Originally the Didcot, Newbury and Southampton Junction Railway (DN&SR) did not pose a particular threat to the LSWR's Southampton monopoly, since it proposed a route from Didcot through Newbury to Micheldever on the LSWR north of Winchester. Parliamentary permission was granted and construction of the section between Didcot and Newbury was begun. Meanwhile to the south there was a re-think. This was spurred partly by the realisation that a direct line to Southampton would be more viable, and also by the support from Southampton, the occupants still desiring a direct link with the industrial north.

Above: A Portsmouth-bound train arrives at Netley in the early years of the 20th century although after the line had been doubled in 1910. The platforms were apparently lengthened up to the road bridge when doubling took place, and the extensions to the up platform can be discerned in this photo. The signal box has yet to be weather-boarded.   (Photo: Lens of Sutton Association)

Therefore, in 1882 a Bill was passed for an extension to Southampton in the face of LSWR opposition, and GWR ambivalence, neither of whom wished to see this independent company succeed. This ran south from Burghclere to the eastern edge of Winchester and then on through Chandlers Ford to Southampton with stations at Chilworth, and Shirley (possibly on a site where the author went to school). It would then travel down what is now Hill Lane, through what was to become The Dell football ground, and across the LSWR between now-renamed Southampton West and the tunnel entrance. Finally, it would have terminated near Bargate Street on a site later occupied by the Pirelli cable works, and now the West Quay Shopping Centre.

Fencing was constructed along the route in Southampton and some work begun. However, increasing financial difficulties hit the Company, and, although the line was opened to Winchester on 1st May 1885, work on the route to Southampton was suspended. Finally a connection with the LSWR was built at Shawford Junction just south of Winchester which opened on 1st January 1891. With this the final major threat to the LSWR's monopoly on lines in Southampton was overcome. However, in truth it was a strategic loss to the railway system of southern England as the DN&SR's role in both World Wars was later to prove, but it suffered from the indifference of both the LSWR and GWR as well as their successors, and never flourished as it should.

To the East, Fareham and Portsmouth

Rather surprisingly the first line that was proposed to reach Southampton from the east was one that was seen as an alternative to the LSWR's mainline to London. In 1845 the Southampton, Petersfield and London Direct Railway (SP&LDR) projected a line running parallel to the LSWR line to South Stoneham where it would branch east through Bishops Waltham to Petersfield. Here it would join the proposed London and Portsmouth Direct Atmospheric Railway. Again the collapse of the first *Railway Mania* put pay to the scheme.

On 19th May 1856 the foundation stone was laid for a new military hospital at Netley. This was a project on a grand-scale with a building a quarter of a mile long which could treat 1000 patients. Not unsurprisingly there were then plans to better link this colossal development with the outside world.

In 1859 the Southampton and Fareham Railway (S&FR) was proposed linking the LSWR line at Fareham to a terminus at Woolston via Warsash, Hamble, and Netley Abbey. Plans were submitted to Parliament but then withdrawn. Then there was a revival of the SP&LDR under the title of the Petersfield Railway, this time running across Southampton Common to a joint terminus with the A&RR, with a capital of £260,000. This scheme was however, never authorised, and similar fates befell other similar proposals.

However, one scheme did come to fruition, the Southampton and Netley Railway (S&NR). This Company was initially independent and proposed a route from the LSWR mainline from St Denis (an earlier name for St Denys) crossing the Itchen on a 140 yard long bridge. It would then have climbed to the top of Lance's Hill before descending to a terminus at the 'end of the public road leading from Hound Church to the Military Hospital at Netley', a distance of some 2.25 miles.

Opposition was surprisingly muted, and the LSWR decided to adopt the scheme, finally absorbing the Company in 1865. By this time the route had been changed, the junction at St Denys now faced south rather than north, and the position of the river bridge had now moved up-stream and the bridge shortened. From here the route now passed close to the bank of the Itchen to Woolston before turning east and regaining the original route near Miller's Pond. This drew objections from the Itchen Bridge Company whose floating bridge plied the Itchen between Woolston and Southampton near the terminus station. Their concerns were overcome when Clause 24 was inserted into the Bill stating that a station would be built at Woolston, and the road from there to Botley be protected.

The railway was opened on 5th March 1866, with stations at Northam Road for Bitterne, Woolston and Netley, a station being opened at Scholing (an earlier name for Sholing) in August the same year. But it was not to be until 1889 when a line was opened connecting Netley with Fareham, thus providing a more direct route between Southampton and Portsmouth. Later, in 1900, a branch was built into the hospital at Netley for ambulance trains.

The Line to Fawley

In the late nineteenth century the Waterside area, as it is now known, to the west of Southampton Water was sparsely populated, and an unlikely target for railway development. However, promoters had other prizes in mind. One of the targets was to take some of the Isle of Wight ferry traffic, such was the aim of the Southampton and Isle of Wight Railway who submitted proposals for a line to Lepe in a Bill in 1861, but this was withdrawn along with Bills submitted in 1862 and 1865.

Later the Swindon, Southampton and New Forest Railway was proposed in 1871. Running to Stone Point near Lepe, where a port would be developed, the possibility of a Solent Tunnel to the Island was also mooted. This later became the Swindon, Marlborough and Andover Railway (SM&AR), which received Royal Assent for a Bill for railways from Swindon to Marlborough and from Savernake to Andover, the line to Lepe being omitted. Later still this became the Midland and South Western Junction Railway (MSWJR), and finally linked Southampton with Cheltenham.

The Stone Point scheme was subsequently revived by the SM&AR under the title of the Isle of Wight Extension Railway, which would have included a triangle at Redbridge. A tunnel to Gurnard Bay on the Island was

extensively discussed, but in the end only the railway to Lepe gained Parliamentary approval in 1882. Sadly the SM&AR had insufficient funds to proceed further. In order to placate the LSWR the SM&AR had proposed joint control for the line, but the LSWR laid down hard terms. This was probably not surprising as it had just been part of a major investment to build the line to Ryde Pier Head on the Island to bolster the ferry traffic on the Portsmouth route, something the proposed tunnel would have undermined.

This was not the end for the prospect of a line to Stone Point, for the scheme was revived again in 1885 under the title of the South Hampshire Extension Railway and Pier Company. (Readers of *Southern Rails on the Isle of Wight Volume One* may recall that this company was mentioned in connection with the development of the line from Merstone to Ventnor Town on the Island). But although the Stone Point line was again authorised under an Act passed in 1886 once more it was never built.

It was left to the LSWR to make the next proposal for a line from Totton to Hythe, Fawley and Stone Point, applying for a Light Railway Order in 1902. This was probably a 'blocking' manoeuvre to prevent further proposals. An order was granted for a line from Totton to Fawley in 1903, but allowed to lapse.

However, the construction of a Refinery at Fawley by the *Anglo Gulf West Indies Petroleum Co.* (AGWI), later part of *Standard Oil*, in the early 1920s led to a revival of the proposal as a joint venture between the Oil Company and the LSWR. However, the line was eventually completed under the auspices of the SR opening on 8th July 1925.

With this the railway system around Southampton in the north, east and west corridors was complete, and the mainlines have served the city largely intact into the 21st century. There were also a number of smaller industrial lines built which will be examined in *Southern Rails on Southampton Docks*. More recent developments have seen most of the mainlines electrified, and while in the docks very little track mileage is left the railways still carry a significant proportion of the traffic passing through them.

The London and Southampton Railway

On 10th June 1839 the first trains ran between Northam (because the station at Southampton was incomplete) and Winchester on the LSWR. As has been noted previously the line was opened in stages commencing in May 1838, and would not be complete until 11th May 1840. However, on this day the locomotive *Pegasus*, a 2-2-2 tender locomotive built by *Tayleur & Co* of Vulcan Foundry in March 1839, hauled trains the twelve miles between the two stations in some twenty-six minutes.

Construction

Construction of the line had not gone smoothly, the original engineer Frances Giles, having to be replaced by Joseph Locke due to the slow progress of the work. Locke in turn gave much of the construction work to Thomas Brassey, but the contractor for the line between Winchester and Southampton was David MacIntosh.

The marshy nature of some of the ground on the approach to Southampton proved something of a challenge. Freeling in his *London and Southampton Railway Companion* states that south of what is now the Dukes Road bridge and north of Mount Pleasant crossing where the line runs along the bank of the River Itchen, the contractor had had to employ methods similar to those used by George Stephenson at Chat Moss. This involved sinking what Freeling termed a 'platform of trees and hurdles loaded with earth and sand' into the mud to provide a foundation. When completed the foundation lay some 16ft below the low water mark, and the 800 yard embankment was then built to a level 5ft above the highest spring tides.

Early Services

From 9th November 1840 the LSWR ran passenger trains on weekdays to Nine Elms departing at 6am, 8.30am, 11am (the fast train), 1.30pm and 6pm. In addition there was an early morning mail train and two goods trains. Stopping trains took 3 hours 46 minutes to complete the journey, while the fast train did the trip in 3 hours.

Fares between London and Southampton were 20s (£1) for the fast train, 18s (90p) for first class on the mixed stopping train with second class passengers paying 12s (60p) for the journey. Meanwhile third class passengers were accommodated on the goods trains at a fare of 7s (35p) for the privilege of riding in an open wagon on a journey that took six hours. There is little doubt that the LSWR did not want to encourage third class class travel!

Because these were still the early days of railway travel the Company clearly felt that they needed to instruct people and allay fears about this new mode of transportation. Therefore, they issued leaflets to every passenger with the regulations for the journey, which contained the reassurance that 'when approaching a curve or gradient, the guard will blow his whistle to warn passengers'. Also that before departure the guard would shout 'Now hold fast please, we are about to start'. Of course as trains were loose-coupled in those days this was probably good advice!

Extensions

The LSWR quickly looked for expansion, indeed the change of name from the L&SR was to facilitate that, particularly with the inhabitants of Portsmouth. As has been seen a number of branches were opened that had an influence in the Southampton area. In addition the opening of the Bishops Waltham branch in 1863, the Mid-Hants line between Winchester and Alton in 1865, and the opening of the mainline beyond Salisbury to Exeter and Cornwall, increased the number of destinations passengers could travel on LSWR metals.

Of course too there were extensive developments in and around London, which will be chronicled in later volumes in this series. However, the most significant development as far as the Southampton to London line was concerned was the extension from Nine Elms to Waterloo opened on 11th July 1848. This took the LSWR to the heart of the capital, and became one of the most famous railway stations in the world.

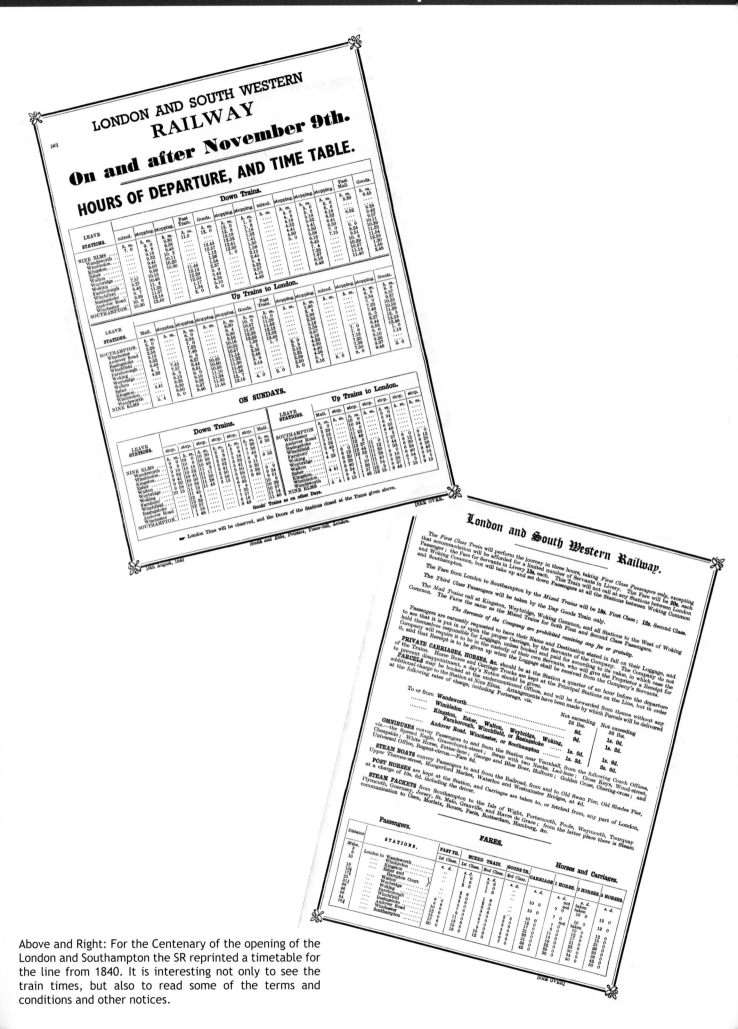

Above and Right: For the Centenary of the opening of the London and Southampton the SR reprinted a timetable for the line from 1840. It is interesting not only to see the train times, but also to read some of the terms and conditions and other notices.

The Route From Southampton Terminus to Airport
Based on 1945 Ordnance Survey Map with Additions

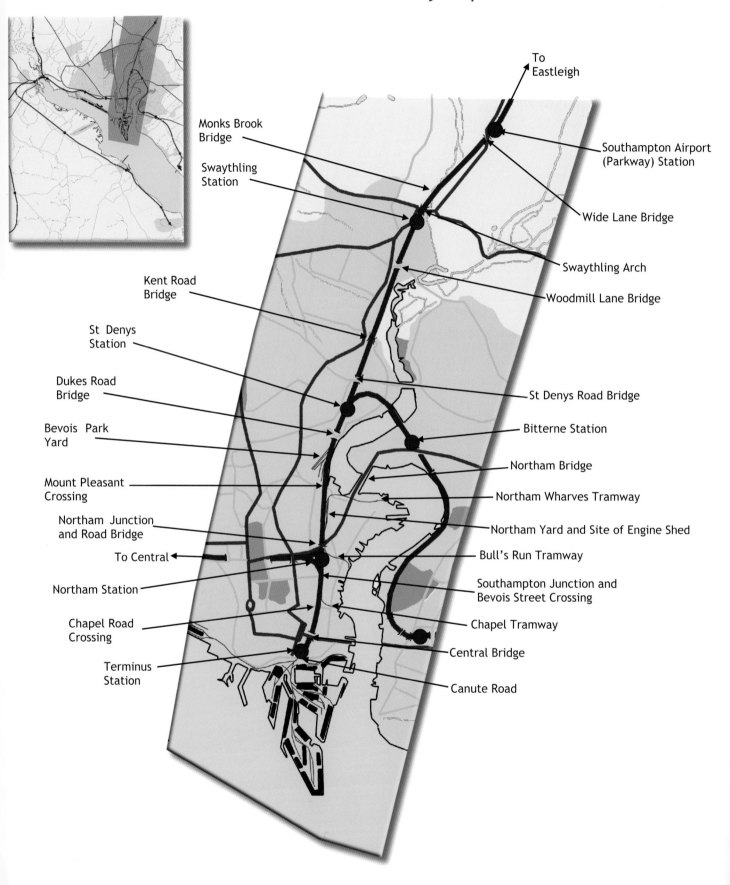

To Eastleigh

Monks Brook Bridge

Swaythling Station

Southampton Airport (Parkway) Station

Wide Lane Bridge

Kent Road Bridge

Swaythling Arch

Woodmill Lane Bridge

St Denys Station

Dukes Road Bridge

St Denys Road Bridge

Bevois Park Yard

Bitterne Station

Northam Bridge

Mount Pleasant Crossing

Northam Wharves Tramway

Northam Junction and Road Bridge

Northam Yard and Site of Engine Shed

To Central

Bull's Run Tramway

Northam Station

Southampton Junction and Bevois Street Crossing

Chapel Road Crossing

Chapel Tramway

Terminus Station

Central Bridge

Canute Road

Left: In the early days of the LSWR third class carriages were little more than trucks with seats, open to the elements. By the 1850s things had moved on a bit, but not much, as this picture of an old grounded third class coach of that period in use as a store at Bitterne station shows.
(Photo: Lens of Sutton Association)

Other Developments under the LSWR

Meanwhile on the line in Southampton there were other developments. The opening of the stations at Northam, St Denys and Swaythling, have already been noted. In 1845 a double needle telegraph system was installed, and in 1865 block signalling introduced between Eastleigh and Southampton. 1858 saw the opening of the new curve at Northam, completing the triangle there, and enabling trains from London to run directly onto the Dorchester line.

A long period of negotiation with the local authority in Southampton led to the replacement of the level crossings at Marsh Lane and Bridge Road with what became known as Central Bridge in 1882. Twenty seven acres of land were purchased from the Bevois Estate in 1893 for £13,200 for what became known as Bevois sidings, which were brought into use on 16th September 1901 and extended in 1907. Quadrupling of the line between Northam Junction and St Denys came into use in

1902. Later in 1903 the engine shed at Northam was closed with the opening of the facilities at Eastleigh, although a shed was maintained in the docks, and servicing facilities at the terminus station.

As traffic increased additional services were provided for passengers on trains. In 1890 *Pullman* coaches were introduced on trains between London and Bournemouth, looking somewhat incongruous in between the non-corridor stock of the time. The LSWR began to build corridor stock from 1903 some of which found its way onto services between London, Southampton and Bournemouth. A supper-car was introduced on the 9.45pm Waterloo to Southampton departure in 1913, serving as a breakfast-car on the return trip the following morning.

World War One

The departure of British forces to France in 1914 saw an extraordinary amount of traffic pass over the LSWR's rails

Right: Swaythling was often used as a place to photograph trains. Here an unidentified Adams 4-4-0 and a Drummond C8 class 4-4-0 head a Bournemouth express. The C8s were built in 1898, and the LSWR stopped using crosses on their headcodes from 1900, and so this photo can be dated to this period. The first four carriages are non-corridor bogie stock with semi-elliptical roofs first introduced in the 1890s with a full brake nearest the locomotives, while the fifth vehicle is a *Pullman* coach, as mentioned in the text.
(Photo: Copyright HMRS H.F.Hilton collection)

in a short period of time. Between 10th and 31st August 1914 670 trains ran to Southampton docks, and it is reported that on one day in September 100 trains ran through to the docks, with minimal disruption to ordinary services.

Surprisingly the hostilities had little effect on the normal operation of the London line, although the length of journeys was increased slightly. In 1918 there were some reductions in services, but these were soon restored when hostilities ceased.

Locomotives

For the opening of the line forty locomotives were ordered from various suppliers, including two locomotives No.40 *Fly* and *Southampton* constructed by *Summers, Grove and Day* at their Millbrook Foundry. Most of these locomotives were 2-2-2 tender locomotives like *Pegasus*. Many of them were not destined to last long in service being quickly replaced by larger, more powerful and reliable, designs.

The first locomotive superintendent of the L&SR is recorded as Joseph Woods, who ordered the initial tranche of locomotives from a variety of private suppliers. He was replaced by John Gooch in 1840, who had previously worked on the Manchester and Leeds Railway. He was responsible for the establishment of a locomotive manufacturing facility at Nine Elms, which was building locomotives when he left the LSWR in 1850. Gooch was succeeded as Mechanical Engineer by Joseph Beattie, who developed some of the iconic early LSWR locomotive designs, including some that were to remain in use until nearly the end of steam.

Beattie was succeeded by his son, William, in 1871, but the son failed to live up to his father's reputation. He 'outsourced' new locomotive construction, rather than coming up with his own innovations, or simply constructed more locomotives to his father's designs. Finally he resigned in 1877 to be replaced by William Adams.

Adams produced many notable designs for the LSWR, among which were the O2 tank locomotives that became so intrinsically linked with the Isle of Wight, as well as tender engines capable of coping with the increasing loads that were the consequence of the developing traffic. Adams was succeeded by Dugald Drummond, (to whom the author is no known relation), in 1895.

Drummond oversaw the establishment of the works at Eastleigh in 1903, a development that will feature in a later volume. He also produced a series of four-coupled locomotives, both tender and tank that proved ideal for the LSWR at the turn of the century. He in turn was replaced as Chief Mechanical Engineer by Robert Urie in 1912, who was responsible for the first really successful series of six-coupled designs for the LSWR capable of handling express trains, as well as mixed traffic duties. Many of the locomotives designed by these last three engineers will feature in these pages.

Under the Southern

At the Grouping in 1923, the LSWR became part of the Southern Railway (SR). The SR completed various works that the LSWR had already authorised including the Fawley branch, already noted, and also the laying out of a marshalling yard at Northam on the site of the old engine shed in 1923. In essence much of the infrastructure on the London line between Terminus and beyond Swaythling did not change significantly under the Southern.

New locomotives were introduced, including Maunsell's *Nelsons*, which along with the Urie-designed *Arthurs* and mixed traffic S15 class, all 4-6-0 tender locomotives, provided the backbone of the mainline services for many years. Four-coupled classes like the Drummond T9s, L11s and L12s handled many of the secondary duties, along with four-coupled tanks such as the Adams T1s and O2s, and Drummond M7s.

A new luxury train, the *Bournemouth Limited* was introduced in 1929, with the all-Pullman *Bournemouth Belle* being seen on the route from 1931. In 1939 a special working of the *Belle* took place on 10th June to celebrate the centenary of the opening of the L&SR. *King Arthur* class *Sir Congreave* ran from Waterloo to Southampton Central in 84 minutes, before making its way to Bournemouth in a further 35.5 minutes. This was under half the time the first trains took to get from Nine Elms to Southampton in 1840.

Boat trains continued to be a major source of traffic for the London line, running into the docks to allow passengers direct transfer onto their ships, increasing when the New Docks were established. An unusual working was the *Flying Boat* or *Imperial Limited* train, introduced on 12th November 1937. This initially ran to No.50 berth at the docks to connect with the *Imperial Airways* Empire Flying Boat services. It consisted of one or two *Pullmans*, attached to the 8.30am from Waterloo, which were detached at Southampton Central or Eastleigh, and hauled into the docks.

During the course of the journey from Waterloo the flight clerk on board had to weigh both passengers and their luggage as part of the check-in procedures. Later, in June 1939, this became a dedicated departure from a private terminal near Airways House in Buckingham Palace Road linked to platform 17 at Victoria station, leaving at 8.05pm. This allowed passengers to overnight at the South Western Hotel. The service continued secretly during the war, running to convey passengers for Hurn airport, and the Poole Flying Boat station, with many 'VIPs' making the trip en-route to various destinations.

The Second World War

The outbreak of the Second World War brought new strains for the railway. Southampton was the major embarkation port at the outbreak of the war in 1939, with 261 troop trains arriving at Southampton between 9th September and 5th October. In the opposite direction it

Above: One bombing incident during World War Two occurred on the line near St Denys when Lord Nelson class No.860 *Lord Hawke* fell into bomb crater on 14th August 1940. (Photo: Courtesy *Southern Daily Echo*)

also handled some of those evacuated from Dunkirk in 1940.

Many children and civilians were also evacuated from London with some travelling as far as Bournemouth on special trains. Southampton, also a likely target for bombing, witnessed an exodus to the countryside, particularly the New Forest.

These predictions proved accurate as Southampton suffered from considerable German bombing, which affected much of the docks and town centre. Other incidents occurred at various points throughout Southampton, which will be detailed later.

On the outbreak of war there were changes to the level of service. The *Bournemouth Belle* was suspended, but restaurant cars were still featured on some express workings in the 1941 timetable. These had disappeared by 1943. However, gradually trains began to run at near pre-war speeds with the 3.25pm departure from Waterloo reaching Southampton in an hour and forty minutes in the winter of 1943.

But the greatest challenge was yet to come, for Southampton was to be the focus of the D-day landings. A huge operation took place both in Southampton and the region surrounding it preparing men and equipment, as well as transporting them to the ships when the time came to embark. That this was done while still maintaining a normal service was some achievement.

However, there was yet another menace to be faced, the 'flying bomb', and once more trains ran between Waterloo and Bournemouth carrying evacuees from the capital. Fortunately this threat proved short-lived, and soon people returned to the capital in time to celebrate the end of hostilities.

Post-war and Nationalisation

The Southern had been battered by the war, but was unbowed, and quickly moved to restore services. On the Waterloo to Bournemouth route the *Bournemouth Belle* resumed operation on 7th October 1946. In 1947 new Bulleid designed coaches were introduced. During the war the first of Bulleid's *Merchant Navy* streamlined 4-6-2 Pacifics began service, and had been well employed on the Waterloo to Southampton line. Now they took regular charge of the *Belle*. They were joined by their smaller cousins, the *Battle of Britain* and *West Country* classes, which, by dint of their lighter weight, had a wider route availability. However, by now Nationalisation was on the horizon.

British Railways took over operation of the Southern's routes on 1st January 1948. At first there was little difference save for some re-lettering of locomotives, but gradually other changes happened. Most striking was probably a short period when an experimental blue livery was applied to some of the Bulleid Pacifics, but soon the green livery for passenger locomotives and black for goods, or mixed traffic locos became the norm. New

Above: A class 74 electro-diesel heads a train composed of a 3-TC and 4-TC electric sets past Bevois Park sidings in August 1968.
(Photo: John H.Bird Copyright SOUTHERN-images)

coaching stock also continued to be introduced.

In the 1950s the first of the BR standard classes began to make an appearance on the line, although many pre-grouping locomotives could still be seen in action. Later many of the Bulleid Pacifics were rebuilt to remedy some of their unreliable features, and at the same time they had their streamlined casings removed, making them not dissimilar in appearance to some of the new standard classes.

Traffic continued at a high level, and the trans-Atlantic boat trade was still well-patronised with many dedicated boat trains being run from Waterloo to the docks. However, the end of steam was coming, in 1957 *Hampshire* diesel-electric multiple units (DEMUs) took over many of the local services in the Southampton area resulting in shorter journey times. Now options were being considered for the future of the London line.

Electrification

It was the *Daily Mail* that announced that the whole of the Bournemouth line was to be electrified, however, the date was 6th November 1936, and their 'scoop' proved somewhat premature. In fairness it is quite probable that had the war not intervened the electrification of the Bournemouth line would have been a logical step. However, it was not until September 1964 that a £15

million plan was announced for electrification from Brookwood, then the limit of the electrified lines, to Branksome, as well as the Lymington branch.

Before this consideration had been given to the type of electrification to be employed on the route, and a plan was produced to use overhead catenary between Waterloo and Weymouth. In the end a reduced scheme was settled on making use of the standard Southern third-rail 750V d.c. system electrifying 90 route miles involving 236 miles of trackwork, as well as the introduction of colour light signalling. In addition a new station was to be opened at Southampton Airport, which came into operation in April 1966.

Work proceeded quickly and on 3rd April 1967 the first passenger-carrying electric train departed from Bournemouth for Waterloo. By then too Southampton Terminus and Northam stations had closed, on 5th September 1966, the last train having departed on 3rd September.

On the rest of the line, steam was still to hold sway for another few months until finally steam operations on the Southern Region came to an end on 9th July 1967. On the 10th July a full electric timetable was operated on the route with VEP (Vestibule Electro-magnetic Brake), REP (Restaurant Electro-magnetic Brake) and non-powered TC (Trailer Control) units, all based on mark 1 stock, making

Above: Steam at St Denys in the 21st century as *Battle of Britain* class No.34067 *Tangmere* heads *The Royal Wessex* charter from Weymouth to London Victoria on 18th June 2005. (Photo: John H. Bird Copyright SOUTHERN-images)

up the trains. The new basic service consisted of a two-hourly fast service, an hourly semi-fast, and hourly slow, with extra services in the peak. Express services took seventy minutes to travel between Waterloo and Southampton.

Passenger numbers increased with the new service, and for many years this provided the settled pattern. The original connection at Northam from the old Terminus to the Bournemouth line was lifted in December 1973. Meanwhile the line from Northam to the docks was singled in 1970.

Control of signalling in the Southampton area transferred to Eastleigh in 1981 resulting in the closure of most of the remaining signal boxes in the area. At Chapel Road the crossing was made open, with the gates replaced with flashing lights without barriers.

In 1986 the line became part of *Network South East*, which resulted in stations being spruced up along the route. Then in 1988 new 442 (*Wessex*) units were introduced on the line in connection with the electrification between Bournemouth and Weymouth.

Privatisation and into the 21st Century

Along with the rest of the railway system the Waterloo-Southampton-Bournemouth-Weymouth route was privatised in 1996, the new operator being *Stagecoach* under the *South West Trains* branding. Another development was the building of the new Southampton Football Ground alongside the tracks at Northam on the site of the former gasworks between 1999 & 2001, sadly no provision was made for fans to travel to the ground by train.

However, in 2003 the site of the former Northam engine shed was chosen by *South West Trains* as the maintenance base for their fleet of class 444 and 450 *Desiro* units. Much of the original trackbed between Northam and Canute Road has now been encroached upon by development. Happily, St Denys and Swaythling stations are still open while the station at the Airport, now renamed Southampton Airport (Parkway), has recently been substantially redeveloped with new facilities.

Southampton Terminus

Above: On 25th July 1966, in the final months of passenger train operations from Southampton Terminus, BR mixed traffic class 4 locomotive No.76061 departs from the station.   (Photo: Copyright Colour-Rail 391499)

On the original opening day of the L&SR between Southampton and Winchester the terminus at Southampton was not ready for use. It finally opened with the rest of the line to Nine Elms on 11th May 1840, with the first passenger train departing for Nine Elms at 6.30am.

The site for the new station was in a region of Southampton called Marsh the name being a clue to the nature of the land. This was undeveloped with fields and cattle grazing nearby as the engraving opposite shows. Six acres of the site had been obtained by the railway from the Corporation in October 1835 for the sum of a guinea (£1.05). However the Corporation obviously felt they had been over generous because when a further parcel of just over an acre of land was required they set a price of £1000. The LSWR took them to adjudication, but lost the case, and ended up paying the legal fees too!

Early Developments

William Tite designed the station building which was built by Nicholson for £10,498. Originally the station boasted two platforms, the southern platform being the arrival road and the north the one used for departures. In addition there was an engine shed, and a goods shed just to the north of the station building. Traffic on the new line exceeded all expectations, and so during the 1840s various improvements were made including better

protection from the weather for passengers, the introduction of fixed signals (these were fitted for gas lighting as opposed to oil in 1854) and a locomotive turntable. 1849 saw the refreshment room both enlarged and licensed for the sale of alcohol, as well as being let to a tenant. Another early development was that the LSWR instigated its own cartage system in and around both Southampton and Nine Elms.

At first the station was named simply Southampton, but in 1858 both it and the station at Blechynden were renamed, Blechynden becoming Southampton West, and the terminus becoming Southampton Docks. This also reflected the significance of the docks to the traffic passing through the station. Capitalising on this traffic land adjoining the station was leased to the *Southampton Imperial Hotel Company* in 1864, and construction of the Imperial (later South Western) Hotel was begun, eventually dwarfing the original station building.

By 1870 the departure platform was 480ft long, with a loading bay of 250ft on the opposite face to the passenger platform, while the arrival platform was 300ft long, the running lines in the terminus still being linked by wagon turntables. There was now a second goods building, 160ft long and 60ft wide, which had been constructed next to the engine shed and adjoining Canute Road. Across Canute Road there were two lines into the docks as well as the connection for the tramway to Town Quay.

Above: An artist's impression of Southampton station in the 1840s. The covered platforms can be seen in the centre, an engine shed on the left. In the right background the station building can be seen.   (Copyright National Railway Museum/SSPL)

North of the station building and original goods shed was the goods yard. Here shunting was still done by horses from a wagon turntable, and so around the edges of the yard were stables, as well as an electric telegraph office. Just to the north of the Bridge Road crossing a ticket platform was provided to allow tickets to be checked on arriving and departing trains (at this time all trains were non-corridor). Loading banks for cattle and goods were provided in 1865 and 1866 respectively.

Meanwhile agreement with the GWR for the running up to four goods and passenger trains between Basingstoke and Southampton in 1866, led to the GWR establishing its own offices and cartage facilities at the station. Later there were to be trains from the North and Midlands, and, from 1874, South Wales and Bristol.

Above: An engraving of the outside of the station shows the rural nature of the setting at Marsh.
         (*Southern Railway Magazine* Copyright National Railway Museum/SSPL)

Right: The view from approximately the same spot in March 2011 with the former South Western Hotel dominating the scene. Not a safe place for sheep to graze.

Left: Trains preparing to depart from Southampton Town and Docks c1910. From the left Adams '415' class *Radial* tank No.131 is departing with a train for Bournemouth via Sway. In the centre T1 0-4-4 tank No.367 waits to depart with a Netley line train. Finally on the right is probably class O2 No.188 with a train of GWR stock for Winchester (Chesil).
(Photo: Lens of Sutton Association)

Early Operations

Some insight into the early operating methods at the terminus can be gained from some reports on accidents in and around the station in the latter half of the nineteenth century. On 9th March 1868 four people were injured when the mail train from Waterloo collided with a goods train near Chapel Road crossing at 11.35pm. The goods train had been allowed to leave the down side siding without a line obstructed message being sent to the signalman working at Southampton Junction (otherwise known as Bevois Street). Block working had been introduced on the line to Bishopstoke in 1865, and down trains were supposed to slow to 10mph at the Bevois Street crossing and then decelerate further to 6mph at Chapel Road crossing for the final approach to the terminus. These slow speeds seem to have prevented a major accident in this case. Later in 1868 new signal boxes were provided at Chapel Road and Marsh Lane, and block working extended to the latter.

Then on 19th December 1886, the 7.45pm from Brockenhurst Junction to Southampton Docks collided with a shunting engine with empty coaching stock between Marsh Lane crossing and the Bridge Road signal box. The passenger train had been running tender-first, but only had one passenger on a four coach train plus break (an early name for brake) van. It was stated that a new overbridge (presumably the Central Bridge erected in 1882) had obstructed the view of the down home signal. What was surprising, was that, despite block working, it was still permitted for trains to be allowed past Chapel Road crossing while shunting was going on. The Board of Trade Inspector blamed the Marsh Lane signalman for lowering his signals when the line was blocked, but also said that the driver of the passenger train should have kept better lookout, and that tender-first operation should be avoided.

The Central Bridge and other Developments

In 1876 a locomotive depot was established at Deanery with a turntable (added later) and coaling facilities.

Electric lighting was employed at the station from 1881. Completion of the Central Bridge in 1882 was the end of a long dispute between the LSWR and the Southampton Corporation. The LSWR first considered the idea of a bridge in 1861. Later, correspondence between the two started in 1871 when the LSWR indicated that they wished to close both the Bridge Road and Marsh Lane level crossings. A census was taken of how long the gates were open for road traffic in 1876, the result of which demonstrated that over six days the Bridge Road crossing was only open for 4 hours 42 minutes! The figures for Marsh Lane were somewhat better, being less affected by shunting within the station, but even so the gates were only open for a little over half the time over the six days.

Still the Corporation were keen to oppose the closure, or at least secure a suitable alternative. So they sought legal advice sending the Town Clerk, Mr. Pearce, to hold a meeting at Bacon's Hotel at Lincolns Inn Fields in London in February 1877. From here he submitted a bill for expenses that included 4s 6d (22p) for port; 10s 6d (52p) for champagne and 3s (15p) for cigars!

A bridge was therefore proposed, but even this took substantial negotiation before agreement was reached in November 1879 for the construction of bridge 50ft wide, which had approach ramps on a 1 in 30 gradient and steps to the Cattle Market. Also agreed was an extension to the Marsh Lane footbridge to maintain the right of way for pedestrians over land acquired by the LSWR to the west of the line from the Corporation as part of the deal. Finally the bridge was opened in July 1882 having been built at a cost of £50,000.

Following its completion and the closure of the Bridge Road and Marsh Lane crossings, as well as St Lawrence Road to the east of the station, a new goods shed was provided on the former line of St Lawrence Road. This was on land acquired from the Southampton Corporation during the 1870s, and in addition five more good sidings were laid.

The early 1890s saw a major rebuilding of the station at

Left: The station building seen from Oxford Street in the early years of the 20th century as indicated by the electric tram. However, the station still proclaims it to be Southampton Docks Station, which it had not been since 1896.

(Photo: Lens of Sutton Association)

Right: Still behind the times as Southampton Terminus continues to display its Southern Railway sign on 14th September 1957.
(Photo: L.Freeman Copyright transporttreasury.co.uk)

Below: Now converted to a casino, the former building has been well preserved as witnessed by this photo from March 2011.

a cost of £3,667, with the addition of a new island platform on the west side, which was known as the excursion platform, and three additional platform roads. The approaches to the station were widened, and there were more goods sidings where the engine shed and 1860s goods shed had been. A new connection was also made into the docks across Canute Road closer to the station, and it is this line that is still in use in 2011. Roofing was also provided over the loading area at the goods shed in 1895. To control the enhanced facilities a new signal box with a 101 lever frame, known as Southampton Yard, was built just south of Central Bridge. Meanwhile, the former ticket platform had been demolished following the opening of Northam station in 1872.

Other Incidents

Two accidents within the vicinity of the Terminus attracted the Board of Trade Inspectors' interest in the 1890s. On 26th May 1892 the first happened when the 5.30pm from Portsmouth to Southampton collided with a coach as it drew into the station. The locomotive was an Adams O2 No.188 built only two years previously (later to be transferred to the Isle of Wight by the SR becoming W23 *Totland*), and was hauling a train consisting of a 3rd class brake, a 1st class coach, a 2nd class, two 3rds and a brake van. It was moving into platform No.1, the furthest south of the platform roads, which was stated to be 200yds long, of which 72yds was under cover and on a curve. Investigations into the causes of the collision found that the driver was given a misleading signal by a traffic inspector, and also that the driver was not making use of the train's continuous brakes.

Another collision occurred on 30th October 1899 which pointed up some more interesting operational methods, when a rake of empty carriages ran into the 1.55pm train from Southampton to Gosport, which was standing in No.6

Above: Not a SR locomotive in sight in this view with a GWR *Duke* class 4-4-0 entering the terminus while on the right a GWR class 2301 *Dean* goods 0-6-0 and an ex-MSWJR 0-6-0 prepare to depart.   (Photo: J.L.Smith Copyright Kidderminster Railway Museum)

platform road ready to depart. Particularly interesting is the fact that the carriages were being shunted by gravity, and that the same disc signal controlled both entry to No.5 and No.6 roads. It was stated that the signalman had not thrown the points in part due to fatigue. This was because a number of troop trains with soldiers heading for embarkation in connection with the second Boer War had passed through the station on their way to the docks that day.

Into the 20th Century

Further improvements came in the early years of the twentieth century when new covered awnings were provided for the platforms in 1906. In addition to LSWR locomotives, MSWJR ones could be seen at the station from the early 1890s with trains from Cheltenham. By the early 1900s there were through services via the MSWJR to places like Bradford, Leeds, Liverpool, Derby and Birmingham. A through Southampton to Manchester coach was provided in 1910, and an improved service offered the following year. By 1914 two express services were offered via the MSWJR, one to Birmingham and the other to Manchester in addition to the Cheltenham services.

Through services via the DN&SR and the Great Central Railway (GCR) to Leicester started from 1901, and by 1903 there was a through service to Newcastle. From 1910 GWR locomotives were also permitted to work through from the DN&SR and so could be seen at the station.

At this point the station had been through two further name changes having been renamed as Southampton Town and Docks in September 1896, and then, in November 1912, Southampton Town for Docks. These changes were presumably meant to clear up misunderstandings as to which Southampton station served which part of the town. However, the station was to have yet another name when following the Grouping the SR named it Southampton Terminus in July 1923, the only station in the country to have terminus in its title.

The South Western Hotel

The building of the Imperial Hotel has been mentioned already, and it opened in July 1867. However, financial problems meant that it soon closed, but in 1870 it was re-opened under the name of the South Western Hotel. In 1882 the LSWR purchased it, and leased it out until 1899 when they took direct control. During the 1920s the hotel was enlarged, which led to a remodelling of the concourse at Terminus, with two platform roads and carriage lines being reduced by 45ft to make room for an access road between the station building and the hotel in 1924.

By 1927 an overall roof had been added across the road, which covered the station concourse. At this point the trans-Atlantic traffic was growing rapidly and many of the rich and famous stayed at the hotel before or after their voyages on one of the great liners or flying boats. However, in August 1940 the hotel ceased to operate, being requisitioned by the Royal Navy. It continued to be used by the Navy and other government departments until 1953, since when it has been used as offices for a variety of users, notably the BBC and *Cunard* for many years. It is now residential apartments.

The Southern Railway

During the latter days of the LSWR it gradually became clear that the West, later Central, station was regarded as the more significant, with the Terminus being increasingly reduced to a secondary role. However, it was still heavily used for both passengers and goods, and various improvements were made to the passenger accommodation in the 1920s.

In 1928 the platforms were renumbered with the north-western most becoming platform one and the rest being numbered through to six. Terminus was also used as a base for staff training, and in 1936 housed an 'O' Gauge model railway representing the route between Northam Junction, Terminus and Central. Being stationmaster at Terminus was of course a responsible position, a post usually occupied by senior people. From 1929 to 1936 Mr. H. Barnes occupied the post. He was succeeded by Mr. H. Holdaway, who held the post until Mr. H.R. Peters was appointed in 1941.

At the outbreak of the Second World War the lines through the station to the docks became busy with troop trains. The station itself was bombed on 23rd November 1940 when much of the town suffered in what became known as the *Southampton Blitz*. It got off relatively lightly with damage to the overall roof, the South Western Hotel and Canute Road crossing box. Some structural damage appears to have been done to the main station buildings, and its upper rooms were little used after the conflict.

Nationalisation

Nationalisation in 1948 brought little real change to the station, except its fortunes were to continue to decline in relation to Central, being increasing used for secondary services. Trains departed for destinations such as Alton, Reading, Fawley, Didcot (via the ex-DN&SR), Cheltenham (via ex-MSWJR), and Winchester City. In March 1949 no fewer than 14 members of the goods staff at the station retired, seven of whom had served the railway for between 42 and 50 years. Times were changing.

There were though some developments at the station. A new 82 lever frame was installed in Southampton Yard box in September 1952, the operation taking ten days, during which time only two platforms were available for use. A new crossing box to control the Canute Road crossing was brought into use in December 1955.

Ticket staff at Terminus were also responsible for issuing tickets for the boat trains. This often involved going to the new Ocean Terminal, or wherever a liner might be berthing, in order to do the booking. In the 1950s and early 60s, there were still considerable numbers of troops passing through the station, and these too had to be catered for.

In 1957 the *Hampshire* DEMUs were introduced. These initially two-car units could carry 127 passengers, and on 16th September took over the route to Winchester City, reducing the journey time by eleven minutes. They then

Above: *Battle of Britain* class No.34064 *Fighter Command* by-passes Southampton Terminus on its way to the docks with a Boat Train on 26th June 1957. Meanwhile, BR class 4 2-6-0 No.76064 prepares to depart from the station.
(Photo: R.C.Riley Copyright transporttreasury.co.uk)

Left: Class T9 No.30707 shunting at Southampton Terminus on 27th August 1960 as seen from Central Bridge, probably making up a parcels train for Portsmouth & Southsea judging from the headcode.

Below: Having passed under Central bridge No.30707 now reverses back to the goods shed. On the left is the platform that served the cattle market, while in the centre Marsh Lane footbridge can be seen.
(Both Photos: P.F.Bloxam)

took over the services to Alton on 4th November.

In 1964 the only direct trains to Waterloo were the Wednesday and Sunday morning Channel Islands Boat Trains, which were advertised as departing from Terminus en-route to Waterloo. However, in fact the train started from the Channel Islands berth in the Old Docks, which caused some confusion.

Closure

By 1965 only an average of 85 trains a day used Terminus, with an average of 1,530 passengers patronising them. Therefore, when closure was proposed there was relatively little opposition to the move. On Saturday 3rd September 1966 the last passenger train pulled out of the station, although it remained in use for parcels traffic until March 1968.

December 1968 saw the local lines being lifted between

Terminus and Southampton Junction. Southampton Yard signal box was closed in December 1970 and demolished in May 1971. During the 1970s the platforms were used for car parking before most of the station was demolished in 1984/5. Now most of the original station site has been re-developed for housing. However, the former South Western Hotel is in use as offices and residential accommodation, while William Tite's station building, having been empty for twenty years, was restored as a night club and is now a casino.

The goods shed on the east side remained in use, latterly by *Pickfords* until 1990. However, since then it has been restored and is now a car park for the surrounding student accommodation. Meanwhile a single line still runs through the site to Canute Road and into the docks. In the past trains crossing Canute Road were supervised by a man with a red flag, and a bell, but in 1981 flashing crossing lights were installed, and another tradition ended.

Above: Under legal regulations locomotives or trains crossing Canute Road had to be protected by a railway worker with a bell and red flag. Here we see that regulation being adhered to as class T9 No.30313 crosses the road on 24th June 1957.
(Photo: R.C.Riley Copyright transporttreasury.co.uk)

Left: The twilight of the traditional goods train in 1974 in front of the goods shed at Terminus. The trucks appear to be full of empty cable drums.

Right: Happily the former goods shed has been preserved and restored, and in March 2011 is in use as a car park. This view is of the road-side of the shed not often seen in pictures of the station.

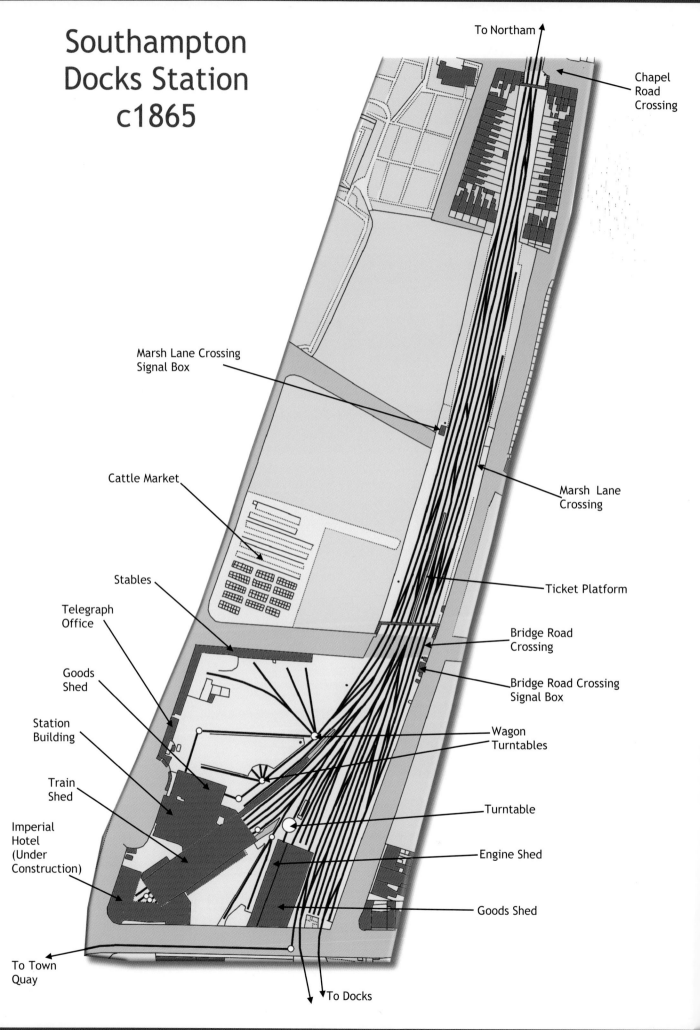

Southampton Docks Station c1865

To Northam

Chapel Road Crossing

Marsh Lane Crossing Signal Box

Marsh Lane Crossing

Cattle Market

Ticket Platform

Stables

Bridge Road Crossing

Telegraph Office

Bridge Road Crossing Signal Box

Goods Shed

Wagon Turntables

Station Building

Train Shed

Turntable

Imperial Hotel (Under Construction)

Engine Shed

Goods Shed

To Town Quay

To Docks

Southampton Terminus c1933

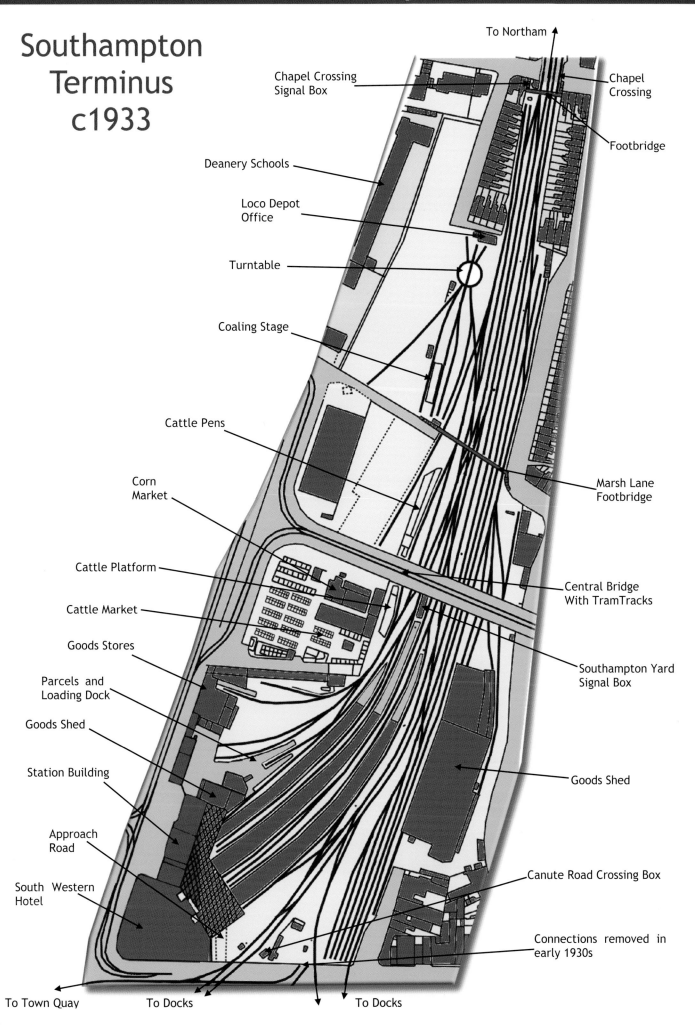

To Northam

Chapel Crossing Signal Box

Chapel Crossing

Footbridge

Deanery Schools

Loco Depot Office

Turntable

Coaling Stage

Cattle Pens

Marsh Lane Footbridge

Corn Market

Cattle Platform

Central Bridge With TramTracks

Cattle Market

Goods Stores

Parcels and Loading Dock

Southampton Yard Signal Box

Goods Shed

Station Building

Goods Shed

Approach Road

Canute Road Crossing Box

South Western Hotel

Connections removed in early 1930s

To Town Quay

To Docks

To Docks

Signal Boxes

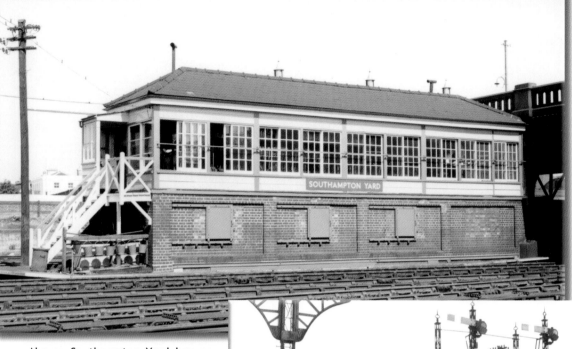

Above: Southampton Yard box on 26th June 1957. This stood next to Central Bridge and was brought into use when the station was remodelled in the 1890s. It was closed on 13th December 1970.
(Photo: R.C.Riley Copyright transporttreasury.co.uk)

Right: The old Canute Road box was probably contemporary with Southampton Yard box, and is seen here on 24th December 1952. It appears to have temporary roofing, probably due to bomb damage as witnessed by the partly demolished wall. (Photo: K.G.Carr Copyright P. Fidczuk)

Left: Probably due to the damage it received the box above was closed on 18th December 1955, and replaced with this box on the other side of the tracks next to the approach road. It is seen here in 1974.

Right: Looking across from Marsh Lane footbridge to the small loco depot at Deanery. B4 class No.30096, now preserved, is shunting, while an M7 is seen just to the right of the loco office. There is a loco on the turntable in the background, and a Mogul is being coaled at the coal stage.
(Photo: R.K. Blencowe collection)

Left: The turntable at Deanery with C14 class 0-4-0 tank locomotive No.30588 being turned. Possibly this was to even out flange wear on the tight curves of the Town Quay route where it was normally to be found at work. It was withdrawn in 1957.
(Photo: Peter T. Hay)

Right: Possibly a forlorn hope when the depot was in operation: A sign on the roof of the derelict loco offices at Deanery asks drivers to avoid disturbing pupils at the nearby Deanery school in 1974.

Left: The concourse at Southampton Terminus is fairly quiet in this view showing the W.H.Smith's kiosk and the row of telephone boxes. The roadway gave access to the entrance to the South Western Hotel.
(Photo: Lens of Sutton Association)

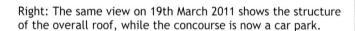

Right: The same view on 19th March 2011 shows the structure of the overall roof, while the concourse is now a car park.

Left: A view of Terminus station just before closure in 1966 from Central Bridge. The former South Western Hotel dominates the background, while just to the right of it the chimneys of the original station building can be seen. A parcels van stands in one of the bay roads. Terminus continued to be used for parcels for a while after it closed to passenger traffic.
(Photo: T.Hastings)

Right: From a similar spot in 2011 the single line that remains to the docks threads its way between the housing and accommodation blocks. The former hotel can be seen over the rooftops, but little else remains in this view.

A City comes to Town

Above and Below: Southampton officially became a city in 1964, however before then it played host to a city, in this case ex-GWR locomotive *City of Truro*, which, following its return to service in 1957, could often be seen at Southampton Terminus on the ex-DN&SR route. *City of Truro* was of course the first locomotive to be officially recorded running at over 100mph, down Wellington bank in Somerset in 1904.

Above: When it was returned to service it was painted into the ornate livery it bore in 1904. It was photographed at Deanery depot at Terminus on an unknown date in the late 1950s. (Photo: B.J.Swain Copyright Colour-Rail BRW249)

Below: Here is No.3440 arriving at Terminus on 24th June 1957. (Photo: R.C.Riley Copyright transporttreasury.co.uk)

Left: Chapel Crossing signal box in 1974. This was of 1889 vintage and a typical LSWR design of the period. It lasted until 1981 when it was closed. On the right hand side of the box is a 'wing mirror' to allow the signalman to observe traffic approaching the crossing.

Below: Chapel crossing on 19th March 2011. The signal box was on the far-side of the line on the left.

Departing from Southampton Terminus a train in the mid-nineteenth century would have passed over Bridge Road crossing, which connected the Town Centre with the Floating Bridge to Woolston. It then passed the cattle platform which backed onto the cattle market. From here the next crossing was at Marsh Lane. Both of these crossings were replaced in 1882 by the Central Bridge which spanned the station approaches just north of the former Bridge Road crossing. The original crossings had their own signal boxes, Marsh Lane being renewed in 1868, which were retained until Southampton Yard box came into operation.

Chapel Crossing

To the west of the line there was still open land, while to the east there was terraced housing and the River Itchen wharves. In later years the loco depot at Deanery was passed, and from 1913 the spire of St Mary's Church could be seen on the left. The next crossing was at Chapel Road. Originally only a small crossing building seems to have been provided here, but by 1866 a footbridge had been constructed on the south side of the crossing spanning the three tracks which crossed the road at this point. There was also a signal box to the north of the crossing on the down side.

A few years later four tracks traversed the crossing, and now the signal box spanned one track on the down side. By 1890 the crossing clearly had become very busy, and there was even talk of turning the road into a subway. This did not happen, but a new signal box did appear on the up side of the line in 1889 with a 31 lever frame, and new crossing gates provided, mechanically worked from the box. The next major re-signalling at Chapel occurred in 1928 when the SR converted the former goods lines into through lines to the docks for the use of boat trains.

Chapel Crossing became one of the last boxes to survive between Northam and Terminus. When Terminus and later Southampton Junction box closed in 1966, the up and down local lines were taken out of use, and Chapel assumed control of Southampton Junction. Then in 1970, when Southampton Yard box was closed, Chapel became responsible for the line down to Canute crossing. Finally the line to the docks was singled in 1980 and the following year, having become the last crossing in the Southampton area to have traditional gates, the crossing became 'open' with flashing lights. The signal box was then closed, although parts of it are preserved at the Swanage Railway.

Left: *Hampshire* DEMU No.1121 approaches Chapel crossing with a train from Alton on 20th June 1966. Note the gasworks in the background.
(Photo: L.Freeman Copyright transporttreasury.co.uk)

Southampton Junction

Moving north from Chapel crossing, the beginning of the Chapel Tramway could be observed to the right. Also on the right the gasworks is seen, and will dominate the skyline on this side until the lines passes Northam Junction. Passing under a footbridge the line now approaches Southampton Junction, the southern-most point on the Northam Triangle. This was the original junction with the S&DR built in 1847.

Just before the junction is Bevois Street level crossing. The original Southampton Junction signal box stood beside the junction north of the crossing on the down side. However, probably in the late 1880s, a new box was built beside the crossing to the same basic design as Chapel Crossing but with a porch. In addition a footbridge was also provided for the crossing.

At first the crossing was double track, but by 1910 a goods avoiding line had been added, and by 1928 four tracks passed over it. The crossing was closed in January 1964, but the box remained in use until after the closure of Terminus. On 2nd October 1966 control of the junction passed to Chapel box, and Southampton Junction box was closed. Finally in December 1973 the old Dorchester line connection was taken out of use, the lines lifted, and

Above: *Hampshire* unit No.1111 passes over the site of Bevois Street crossing and past Southampton Junction box heading towards Terminus with a train from Winchester during the last days of trains to Southampton Terminus. Again note the 'wing mirror'.
(Photo: Copyright Colour-Rail 21736)

Northam

Above: *West Country* No. 34101 *Hartland* rounds the curve towards Southampton Central with a Bournemouth line train. Behind the locomotive can be seen the station buildings spanning the tracks at Northam station. This photograph was taken on 5th April 1965. No.34101 was withdrawn in July 1966, and is preserved at the North Yorkshire Moors Railway.   (Photographer Unknown)

A station was considered at Northam in the 1840s, when it was proposed to build a central station here at the junction of the Dorchester line, and that down to the docks. However, this did not happen until the 1860s when there was a successful campaign for a station in the area. Finally on Sunday 1st December 1872 the station opened. But even then platforms were only built on the lines to and from the terminus, meaning that passengers for the direct services to the west still had to travel to Southampton West.

Given its complex setting in the middle of the triangle of the lines to St Denys, Docks, and West stations, the station was

London and South Western Ry.
—
FROM WATERLOO TO
787
NORTHAM

very basic with two platforms with individual entrances from the road bridge. On the up platform was a waiting room supplied in 1875, while a ladies waiting room was approved in 1880. In 1876 the platforms were lengthened. J. Bull & Sons were the contractors for the station, as they were for many other projects in the Southampton area, their works being nearby. In partial justification for the new station, the LSWR required all down trains to stop here for ticket inspection, the ticket platform at the terminus being abolished at the same time. Roofing for the stairs to the platforms was approved in 1892, and the down platform extended once more in 1897.

When the station was built there were very few buildings in the immediate vicinity. The Ordnance Survey map of 1881 shows the station surrounded by open ground. However, by 1897 the land to the west had been built on. To the east there were the beginnings of a northern extension to the gasworks, which previously had been confined between Bevois Street and Chapel Road. By 1910 the gasworks occupied the whole of the eastern side of the Northam triangle. However, the centre of the triangle remained as allotments.

On several more occasions there was talk of making Northam the site of a new central station north of the

Left: Probably the oldest photo of Northam known shows the stationmaster posing on the up platform. Behind is the original station building and Northam Road bridge. Through the arch of the bridge Northam Junction signal box can be seen in its original position, with the lines from Southampton West curving in from the left. On the left is a poster advising that the Waterloo and City line is now open, which probably dates this photograph to 1898. Note also the calling-on arm on the starter signal marked 'Engine Shed' for access to Northam Engine Shed.
(Photo: Kidderminster Railway Museum)

Right: The view from the down platform showing the shelters on both platforms as well as the original station building and entrance.
(Photo: Lens of Sutton Association)

Left: The date of this photograph is 1908 when the road bridge is being re-constructed, and the original entrances demolished. On the left can be seen the footbridge which was built across the lines to Southampton West to allow pedestrian access to the station during the re-building. Note through the bridge that Northam Junction signal box has now been moved back, with the tracks being slewed to the right as compared with the top photograph. This was to allow the curve to West station to be eased. Below the bridge are the starting and distant signals (distant signals being painted red at that time).
(Photo: Kidderminster Railway Museum)

Right: Drummond-designed K10 class, or *Small Hoppers* as they were known, No.142 built in 1902 pulls into Northam with a train for Alton. The length of the down platform was to allow ticket checks to take place on non-corridor trains before they reached the terminus. The fine gas lamps are also worthy of note, of course the gas didn't have to come far with the gas works just off to the left.
(Photo: Lens of Sutton Association)

Left: On 3rd September 1966, the last day of passenger services at Northam. *Berkshire* DEMU No.1129 pulls into the station with a train from Alton as denoted by the '16' headcode. Note the roof on the up shelter has been replaced by a 'flat-roof', while the roof on the down shelter has been renewed. The *Berkshire* units were a later build of *Hampshires*, constructed in 1962, with some detail differences. The inverted black triangle denoted that that end was the power car and luggage compartment.

(Photo: John H.Bird Copyright Southern-Images)

junction, but this came to nothing. Around the turn of the century a goods avoiding line was built to the east of the station. Then in 1908 the road bridge was rebuilt, and the original entrances to the station demolished. A temporary wooden footbridge was erected, which crossed the lines to Southampton West from an entrance on Northam Road west of the replacement bridge. Then a new station building was built over the line beside the new road bridge, and a pedestrian entrance made from the road between the spans.

From then on little changed at Northam through its Southern and British Railways days. However, the numbers of trains calling there reduced, due to the lessening importance of the route to Terminus. By 1965 a mere 530 passengers are recorded as using the station daily. Given that it only served the lines to Terminus it was inevitable that when that station closed, so would Northam. The last trains called at the station on 3rd September 1966. The station was demolished in 1969-70.

Now the site is dominated by the new St Mary's Stadium of Southampton Football Club. A footbridge has been built across the lines to Southampton Central, as well as the remaining line to the docks and siding for the train depot, for pedestrians to walk over to the new stadium. It seems a pity that money was not invested in a new station at Northam to provide the football fans with direct access to the ground from the surrounding area.

Northam Junction

Moving north from Northam station itself, the train now traverses Northam Junction. This was added in August 1858 to allow trains from London direct access to the Dorchester line, and is on a sharp curve originally with a 7mph speed limit. At the junction on the down side of the line stood the original signal box. Behind the box ran the tramway to Belvidere works, which became known as the Bull's Run, or later the Dibles Wharf tramway, the history of which will be explored in *Southern Rails on Southampton Docks*.

The original Northam Junction box seems to have been replaced in the 1880s by a standard LSWR design. This box even survived being moved back several feet in the early twentieth century as part of a plan to provide additional running lines between the junction and St Denys, which came into use in 1902. Northam curve was eased at the same time. However, this box was finally replaced in July 1923 when the junction was re-modelled. In conjunction with this a new marshalling yard and other sidings on the site of the old Northam engine shed was added. The 56-lever frame from the old box was used in the new one.

Over the years Northam Junction has been altered on a number of occasions. In recent years changes were made when the line to Terminus closed in 1966, then again when the line to the docks was singled in March 1980. This coincided with work to ease Northam curve which was completed in the April allowing the speed restriction to be raised to 25mph. Finally Northam Junction box was closed on 11th October 1981.

Northam Yard

Going north from the junction again there was open land up until the 1880s, but by 1897 development had occurred on either side of the line. In 1870 a siding existed to *Mulford's* timber yard to which others were subsequently added. By 1933 they were a set of north-facing sidings, known as the Mulford sidings, and separate to what was to become Northam Yard.

Journeying towards St Denys once more the site of Northam shed is on the down side of the line. This was a 14 road shed opened in October 1840, and accessed from trailing connections on the down line. Here there was a turntable which was moved further north to occupy part of the site of some old coke ovens, as well as a coaling platform. In the shed there were facilities such as a fitting shop and a smithy. With the opening of the works at Eastleigh in 1903, the shed closed and was demolished. The turntable was removed, but it seems as if the old shed roads remained as a goods yard.

Northam Station in 1908 and 1933

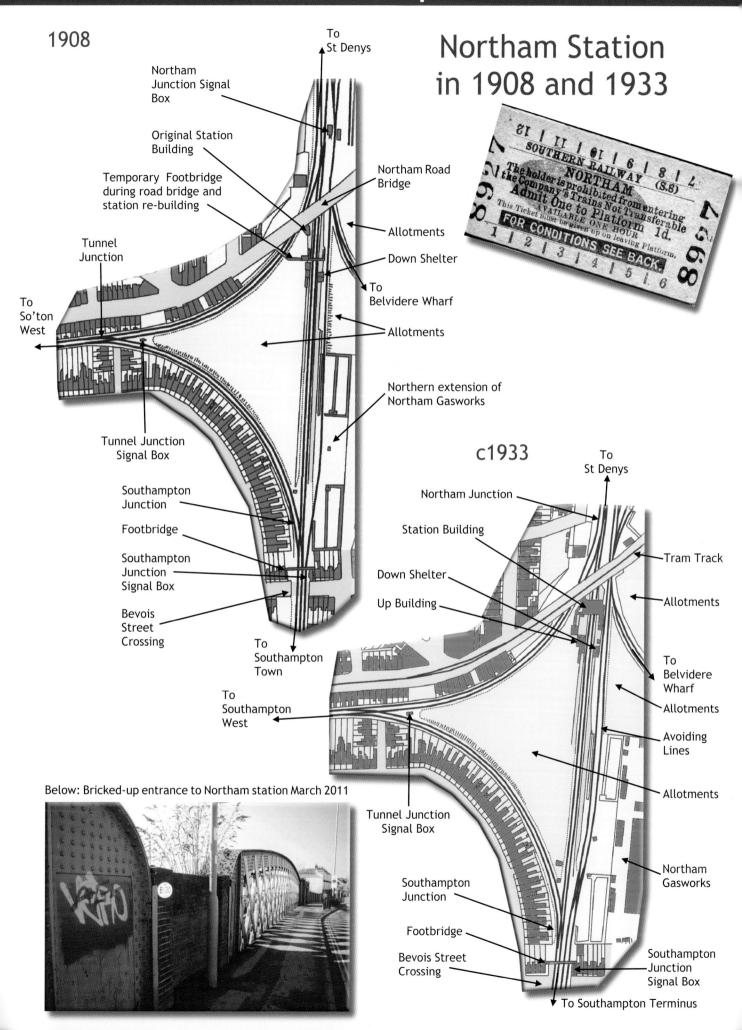

1908

- To St Denys
- Northam Junction Signal Box
- Original Station Building
- Temporary Footbridge during road bridge and station re-building
- Tunnel Junction
- To So'ton West
- Northam Road Bridge
- Allotments
- Down Shelter
- To Belvidere Wharf
- Allotments
- Northern extension of Northam Gasworks
- Tunnel Junction Signal Box
- Southampton Junction
- Footbridge
- Southampton Junction Signal Box
- Bevois Street Crossing
- To Southampton Town
- To Southampton West

SOUTHERN RAILWAY
NORTHAM (S.8)
The holder is prohibited from entering the Company's Trains Not Transferable
Admit One to Platform 1d.
AVAILABLE ONE HOUR
This Ticket must be given up on leaving Platform.
FOR CONDITIONS SEE BACK.
1 | 2 | 3 | 4 | 5 | 6

c1933

- To St Denys
- Northam Junction
- Station Building
- Down Shelter
- Up Building
- Tram Track
- Allotments
- To Belvidere Wharf
- Allotments
- Avoiding Lines
- Allotments
- Northam Gasworks
- Tunnel Junction Signal Box
- Southampton Junction
- Footbridge
- Bevois Street Crossing
- Southampton Junction Signal Box
- To Southampton West
- To Southampton Terminus

Below: Bricked-up entrance to Northam station March 2011

On the up side of the line here a siding was established in 1897, along with a crane and loading dock. This was removed when the line was quadrupled in 1902.

In 1922 the LSWR authorised the redevelopment of the whole of Northam yard. This was eventually carried out by the SR, coming into use in 1923, and remained in use into the 1990s. In later years it provided a base for *Blue* *Circle Cement* who built a depot there with large silos. Having lain out of use for some years it was chosen by *Siemens* as a maintenance depot for their *Desiro* trains, which operate on *South West Trains*. This is now one of the largest buildings in Southampton and clearly visible from many miles up in the sky, having been opened in 2003. Once more the servicing of trains has returned to Northam after a break of a hundred years.

Left: Northam Junction signal box in the late 1960s. This box dates from 1923 when Northam yard was laid out and was built on the up side of the line opposite the site of the box it replaced.
(Photo: Lens of Sutton Association)

Above: On 3rd September 1966 an unidentified class 33 takes the curve towards Southampton Central. This was the last day of services to Southampton Terminus and soon all scheduled trains would take that route. On the right are Mulford sidings with Northam Yard in the distance with the *Blue Circle* silo.
(Photo: B. Townley)

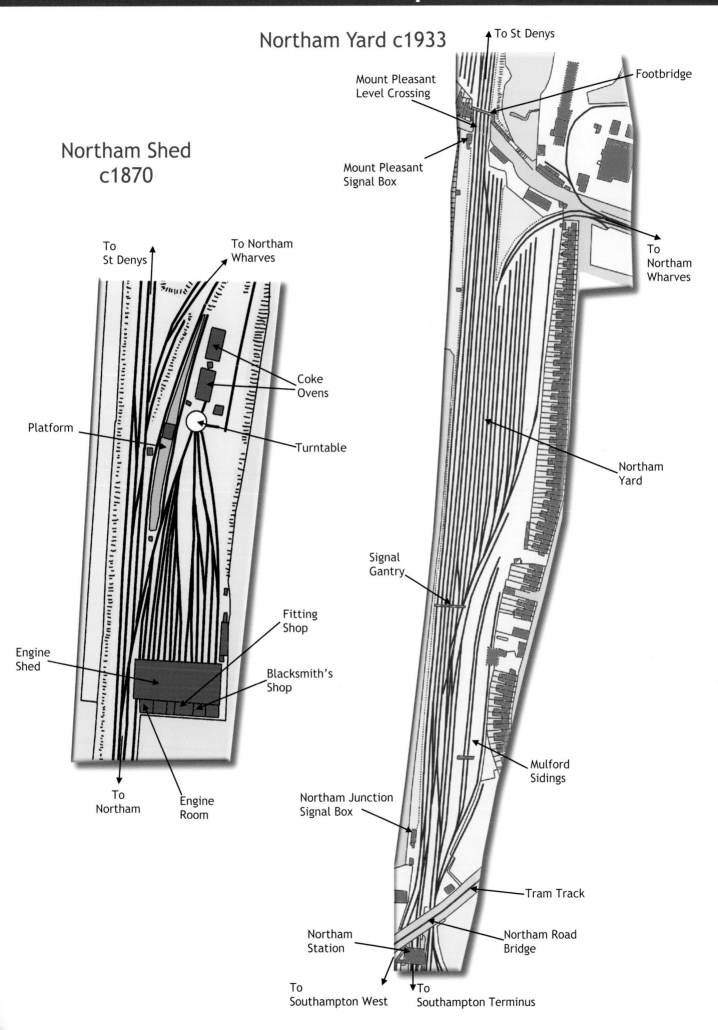

Northam Yard c1933

To St Denys

Mount Pleasant
Level Crossing

Footbridge

Mount Pleasant
Signal Box

To
Northam
Wharves

Northam Shed
c1870

To
St Denys

To Northam
Wharves

Coke
Ovens

Platform

Turntable

Northam
Yard

Signal
Gantry

Fitting
Shop

Engine
Shed

Blacksmith's
Shop

Mulford
Sidings

Northam Junction
Signal Box

To
Northam

Engine
Room

Tram Track

Northam Road
Bridge

Northam
Station

To
Southampton West

To
Southampton Terminus

Left: Photos only seem to exist of parts of the Northam engine shed, usually in the background of photographs of locomotives, such as this one of *Falcon* class No.82 *Sultana* from the mid 19th century.   (Photo: B.Moody collection)

Below: Long after Northam shed had gone U class No.31793 passes Northam yard on 1st September 1959 with a train for Portsmouth & Southsea.

(Photo: P.F.Bloxam)

Left: On 19th March 2011 *Desiro* class EMU No.444012 approaches Mount Pleasant crossing. Behind it the site of Northam shed and Northam yard is now *Siemens'* servicing depot for the *Desiro* units employed by *South West Trains*. On the right is the site of Mount Pleasant signal box.

Mount Pleasant Crossing

When the line was built Mount Pleasant was very much a backwater, with the old farmhouse just a few yards down the road, which still exists as a pub. It was, therefore only provided with a simple crossing manned by a gatekeeper, who would be warned by bells of approaching trains, to close the gates. In 1891 local residents petitioned the LSWR that, in view of increasing traffic at the crossing as the area developed, a full set of gates be provided as had recently been installed at Chapel crossing.

The LSWR seems to have seen the wisdom of their request for in January 1893 an agreement was made with the Corporation for the crossing to be widened to four tracks. A footbridge was also to be built on the north side, and a signal box on the down side. However, sadly the agreement was not enacted before a fatal accident occurred on the crossing in June 1894.

Later, in October 1894 the footbridge was constructed allowing for two extra tracks to the west of the existing ones. The signal box was in service by 1897, but on the up side of the line south of the crossing. Originally the crossing gates were manually operated, but later motors were added to assist the signalman. In 1902 the new running lines came into use, and the box also controlled the southern access to Bevois Park sidings.

On 2nd July 1967 the crossing gates were replaced by lifting barriers, and the track layout for the access to Bevois Park sidings was altered in 1970. Finally the box was taken out of service on 11th October 1981 and demolished shortly thereafter.

Left: Mount Pleasant signal box seen from the footbridge over the crossing after barriers had been fitted to the latter in 1967. (Photo: Lens of Sutton Association)

Below: The interior of Mount Pleasant box in 1980. (Photo: G. Wheeler)

Left: Mount Pleasant crossing looking north on 27th December 1965.
(Photo: Copyright Bluebell Railway Museum Archive-J.J.Smith collection)

Bevois Park Sidings

Travelling north from Mount Pleasant, the line originally crossed a stream, which acted as a drain for an area of marshland. The railway then traversed the marsh on the embankment mentioned on page 14. By 1897 the land to the west of the railway had been drained, and was being used for allotments with the original bridge filled in and the stream diverted into a culvert.

Back when the line opened, Freeling's *London and Southampton Railway Companion* stated that across the river one could observe the 'wood crowded heights dotted with villas, reflected in the river below', as well as the five arches of Northam bridge. Things look a little different today!

On the up side of the line the allotments at Bevois Park were displaced at the turn of the twentieth century, first by two sidings laid in 1897, and then by a new marshalling yard brought into use on 16th September 1901, being later extended in 1907. The yard could be accessed from either the north or south end, and loops were provided to allow the release of engines.

In 1933 some sidings were lengthened and others were removed. In addition, Bryant Quarries established a tar macadam plant there. During World War Two two additional sidings were added.

By 1968 traffic flows were reduced and so some sidings were lifted, however the *Tunnel Cement Company* established a depot there, followed by the *Rugby Portland Cement Company* in 1980. Traffic through the yard was declining by 1990, and ten years later the yard was out of use. It has since been largely lifted save for the retention of two loop lines for engineering use.

Dukes Road Crossing

Next on the journey north came Dukes Road crossing. Like Mount Pleasant, Dukes Road crossing, or St Denis crossing as it was then known, lay in a rural location, and had been an occupation crossing. Later it was provided with two crossing keepers due to increasing traffic, but the inadequacy of this arrangement was shown by an accident in January 1865, when a train hit a cart crossing the line killing the cart's driver.

The immediate cause was that the duty crossing keeper had gone to the toilet, a gatehouse not being provided until later in 1865. He also possessed no watch, and there was no advance warning of approaching trains, other than their whistling. As a result he failed to close the gates to prevent the cart and its occupants from crossing, despite shouting to them. An inquest jury returned a manslaughter verdict, but they also called on the Company to improve the crossing.

However, substantial improvements did not come until the 1890s. In 1893, as part of the same agreement with the Corporation about Mount Pleasant mentioned previously, it was also agreed that the crossing at the now named Dukes Road crossing should be widened to four tracks. A new footbridge would also be provided on the south side of the crossing, and a signal box built on the up side.

Above: Drummond designed T9 class No. 302 passes Bevois Park sidings in the last days of the Southern with a train from Portsmouth & Southsea for Salisbury. There is a fine array of signals with two sets for the down slow and fast lines with home signals for Mount Pleasant and distants for Northam Junction. The calling-on signals on the lower bracket are for Northam Yard. The road is set and signalled for the train to go round the curve at Northam to Southampton Central. (Photographer Unknown)

Bevois Park Sidings
c1933

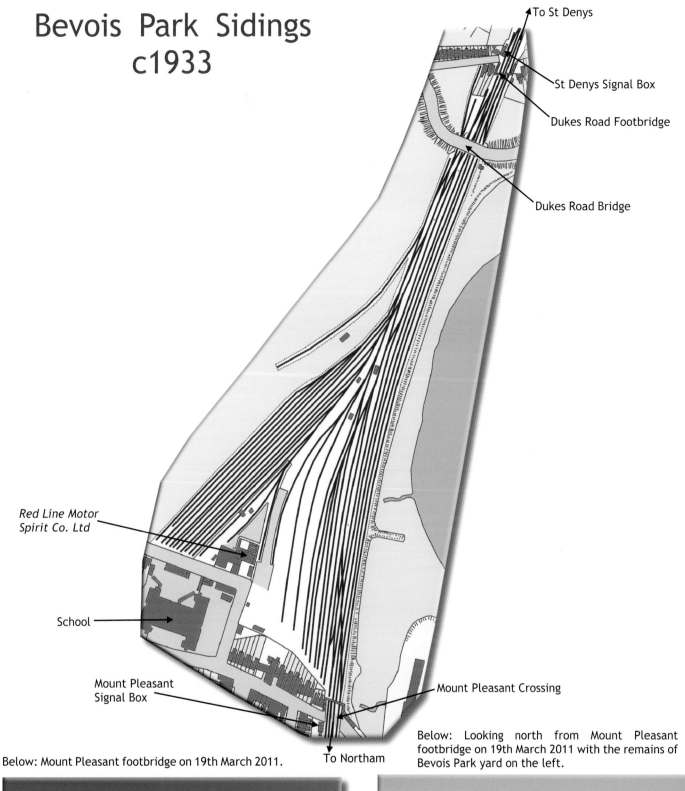

To St Denys

St Denys Signal Box

Dukes Road Footbridge

Dukes Road Bridge

Red Line Motor
Spirit Co. Ltd

School

Mount Pleasant
Signal Box

Mount Pleasant Crossing

To Northam

Below: Mount Pleasant footbridge on 19th March 2011.

Below: Looking north from Mount Pleasant footbridge on 19th March 2011 with the remains of Bevois Park yard on the left.

Right: Copy of a lease agreement drawn up in April 1933 between the SR and L.W. Bryant (Quarries) Ltd to permit the building of a tarmacadam plant at Bevois Park. Special arrangements for the transfer of traffic to these sidings were listed in the 1934 operating instructions.

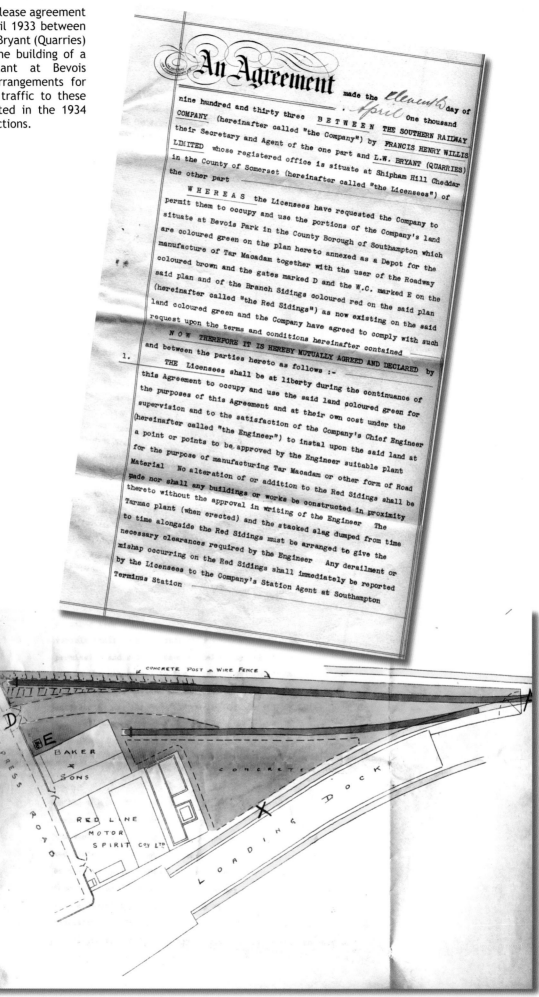

Right: Looking north from Dukes Road footbridge. A train from Waterloo for Bournemouth West via Sway is approaching having passed through the reconstructed St Denys station. The telegraph poles are a feat of engineering in themselves!
(Photo: Lens of Sutton Association)

All this was in place by 1897, with a signal box to the same design as Mount Pleasant, but backing onto the former crossing keeper's house. The box was then known as Dukes Road, although this was probably changed to St Denys in 1899 when St Denys station was rebuilt. However, only two tracks traversed the crossing at this time, but there was room for another running line to be added each side.

In 1901 the Corporation wanted to extend the tramway system, and one option they looked at was to extend the system along Dukes Road and Adelaide Road. They therefore requested the LSWR to build a bridge at Dukes Road. Eventually a complicated agreement was reached, which was signed in the December. As part of which the LSWR would build the bridge, and in return the Corporation would remove the tram tracks from Canute Road, permitting the LSWR to lay up to four new tracks

across the road into the docks.

The new bridge was built on a horseshoe arrangement south of the old crossing. This came into use in 1903 when the crossing was closed, by which time the line to Northam had been quadrupled. Ironically having gone to all this trouble of getting a bridge built the Corporation never extended the tramway via Dukes Road, routeing it instead via St Denys Road.

St Denys box controlled not only the junction with the Netley line, but also the northern connections to Bevois Park yard, and had a 56-lever Stevens frame. Along with Mount Pleasant, it became one of the busiest boxes in the Southampton area. Over the years various changes took place until Eastleigh box took over control of the area in 1981, and St Denys box closed on 11th October.

Above: The signalman watches the photographer from St Denys box on 2nd July 1966. This view clearly shows how the box was built abutting the former crossing keeper's house, which was later demolished leaving the box standing alone.
(Photo: Copyright Bluebell Railway Museum Archive-J.J.Smith collection)

Right: Inside St Denys signal box shortly before closure in 1980.
(Photo: G.Wheeler)

Below: In May 1975 the junction and entrance to Bevois Park sidings at St Denys was relayed, and here the work is underway on 3rd May 1975.
(Photo: R.Newman)

St Denys

Above: On 3rd September 1966 *West Country* No.34040 *Crewkerne* passes through St Denys on the down London line. Note the train indictor board on the right advertising that the next train would be for Southampton Terminus. This was the last day of passenger operation to Terminus, and so one of the last times the staff would have to insert that board into its slot.

(Photo: B.Townley)

Development of local stations in the Southampton area, as in the case of Northam, often came as a result of local agitation for a more convenient way to access the railway. This was helped when the LSWR felt threatened from potential encroachment by other railways into the town, and so wished to curry favour with the population.

Therefore, the first mention of a station at St Denys comes in the LSWR minutes of 16th September 1858, when it was agreed to build a 'short train station' at Portswood in response to a petition received by the Railway from a public meeting held the previous year. However, nothing seems to have happened as a result. Later, on 2nd February 1860, around the time that various proposals were being made for new lines into the town from the east, some of which would have come near Portswood, it was agreed to build a 'temporary' station at Portswood, but again nothing appears to have actually been built at this stage. However, on 28th February 1861, the LSWR noted that a Portswood station could strengthen their position in fighting off opposition in Southampton. It was also at this meeting that the LSWR re-considered their opposition to the proposed Southampton and Netley Railway. So on 1st May 1861 a wooden station was opened on land apparently donated to the LSWR just north of St Denys Road bridge.

It is recorded that single fares from the new Portswood station to Southampton Docks, two miles distant, were 4d first class, 3d second, and 2d third. Seven up trains called at the station on weekdays, and five down. On three of the up trains connections could be made at Bishopstoke for London, but there was only one down connection. However, the new station was destined to have only a short, but eventful, life.

On the 6th December 1861 the then stationmaster, Mr. Noakes, heroically sacrificed his life in saving a woman from being run over by a down train. Tragically he was caught by the engine as he pushed the woman, the wife of another railway employee, out of the way and was killed. Later the Railway was successfully sued when a passenger fell onto the line having stepped onto a broken piece of the platform. In 1862, however, gas lighting and a waiting room were provided.

By 1864 it was agreed that the new line to Netley would form a junction with the mainline just south of Portswood station on a south facing junction. It was therefore decided to move Portswood station south of the new junction and build permanent facilities there.

As a result by the time of the Netley line's opening a

Right: Adams '415' class radial tank No.169 pauses at St Denys with a local train from Waterloo to Southampton at the beginning of the 20th century, after the station had been rebuilt. Note the tall post with co-acting signals on the up London line starter.
(Photo: Lens of Sutton Association)

Left: The square windows on the cab front of the Adams '445' class 4-4-0 No.454 tender locomotive dates this shot to prior to 1909 when the locomotive was re-boilered. It is seen here at platform four at St Denys with a train from Portsmouth via Netley. The carriages are in the classic salmon and chocolate livery.
(Photo: Lens of Sutton Association)

station building had been built on the up side. This was to the same design as Woolston and Netley, the latter being an enlarged version, with echoes of the building at Terminus, except it was not covered with stucco. The rest of the station before 1899 consisted of two platforms, with a waiting room on the down platform, and a footbridge erected across the platforms in 1883 to permit a right of way for pedestrians across the station. A coal siding was added in 1870, additional waiting rooms in 1880, and a further siding in the 1885.

The platforms were lengthened in 1889 as part of the preparations for the opening of the Netley and Fareham line. At first too there was a signal box adjacent to the junction, but, in 1891, the junction was moved slightly south, with a signal box at the north end of the up platform. In 1876 the station was renamed St Denys, in order to avoid confusion with Portsmouth.

With increased traffic on the London line, and the route to Fareham, it was felt necessary to increase the facilities at St Denys. Therefore, a remodelling of the station took place in 1899 at a cost of £9,784. The junction was moved south of the station, and the down platform was extensively rebuilt as an island platform and extended north, with new brick-built waiting rooms and other facilities as well as canopies provided. At the same time a new platform was built to the east of the station for Netley services towards Southampton, again with its own

brick-built waiting room, and the former up platform was extended south, with the signal box being removed. The goods yard was controlled by a ground frame. At the same time the footbridge was also extended to provide a right of way across the whole station, and the platforms were numbered one to four from west to east.

The new facilities brought increased services, and St Denys became one of the places to watch trains in Southampton, with express trains on the Waterloo line either heading down to or coming up from the docks, or onto the route to Bournemouth. Meanwhile local services headed to numerous destinations, not only on the London line and its branches, but also to Fareham and Portsmouth as well as Romsey and Salisbury. Trains to Bristol also called at the station. In 1909 some 300 train movements could be seen passing through the station each weekday.

During the life of the Southern no significant changes were made to the station. Mr. H.Cooper was appointed stationmaster in 1925, remaining in charge until 1945.

South of the station the quadruple lines to Northam came to an end, and on the up side for many years there was a sand drag, to prevent trains from running onto the mainline in front of on-coming trains. In August 1939 D15 class No.467 found itself in the sand, when it was heading a train from Salisbury to Portsmouth. Its driver mistook

Left: Adams A12 *Jubilee* class 0-4-2 tender locomotive No. 623 at St Denys with what appears to be a GWR train from Winchester Cheesehill (or Chesil) to Southampton after the Grouping in 1923.
(Photo: Lens of Sutton Association)

On 14th July 1969 the goods yard was closed, and in September the track lifted. In May 1975 a new track layout came into use south of the station, and the sand drag was removed.

the main home signal for the local home, and tried to advance through the crossing.

Under British Railways two further incidents involving the sand drag were reported. The first was on 29th October 1959 when the driver of the 6.30pm Weymouth to Waterloo train, headed by *West Country* No.34020 *Seaton,* misread the signal and ran through the sand drag into the platform ramp. Just over a year later, on 12th December 1960, rebuilt *West Country* No.34022 *Exmoor,* on a Cardiff to Brighton train, ended up in the same place for the same reason. Fortunately in these cases there appears to have been only slight injuries and damage to the locomotives.

Hampshire DEMUs began to take charge of most of the Netley line services, as well as local services to Winchester and Alton on the London line. Perhaps surprisingly it was not until 1967 that electric lighting was used at the station, gas lighting having held sway until then. This of course coincided with the electrification of the London line, and the appearance of electric multiple units.

A major change during the 1980s was the demolition of the houses to the west of the station, to make way for a new link road that was to run alongside the line between Dukes Road bridge and Swaythling station. This also involved the building of a new approach road to the station called Drummond Drive, and the extension of the footbridge over the new link road in 1987.

By 1988 class 155,156 and 158 *Sprinters* were running services on the Netley line, but these were to be replaced on some routes by electric units with the completion of the electrification of the line in May 1990. In that year the 1866 building was let for office space, being now known as *Drummond House*. Today, the station is still very busy with services to a variety of destinations, a big contrast with the 'temporary' station erected in the 1860s.

Right: The bookstall at St Denys.
(Photo courtesy *Southern Daily Echo*)

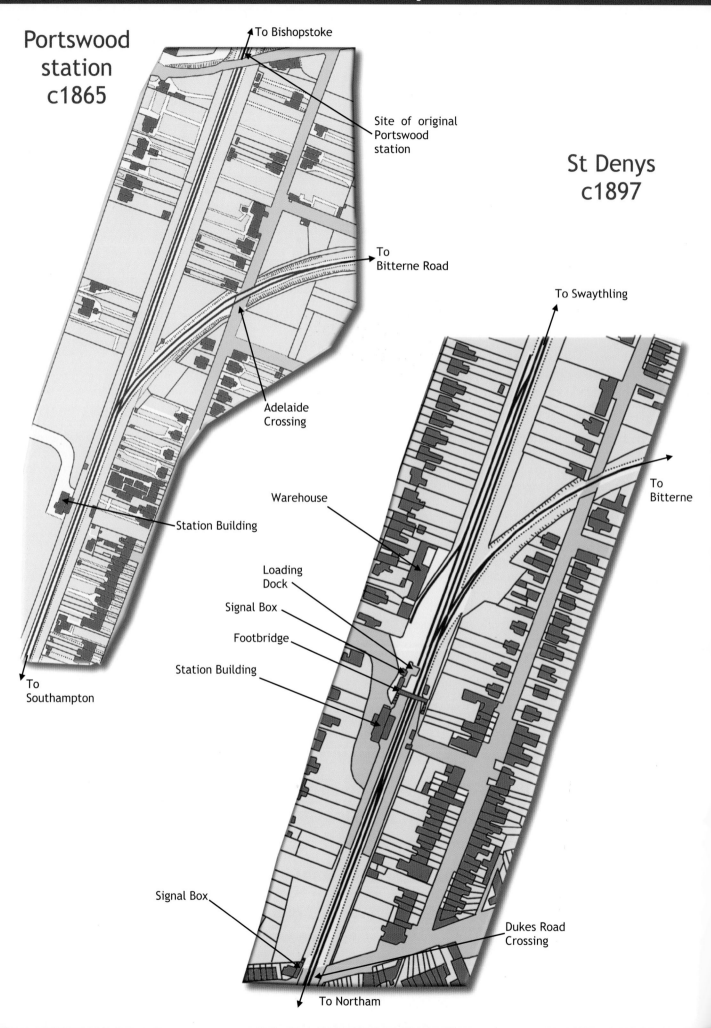

Portswood
station
c1865

To Bishopstoke

Site of original
Portswood
station

St Denys
c1897

To
Bitterne Road

To Swaythling

Adelaide
Crossing

Warehouse

To
Bitterne

Station Building

Loading
Dock

Signal Box

Footbridge

Station Building

To
Southampton

Signal Box

Dukes Road
Crossing

To Northam

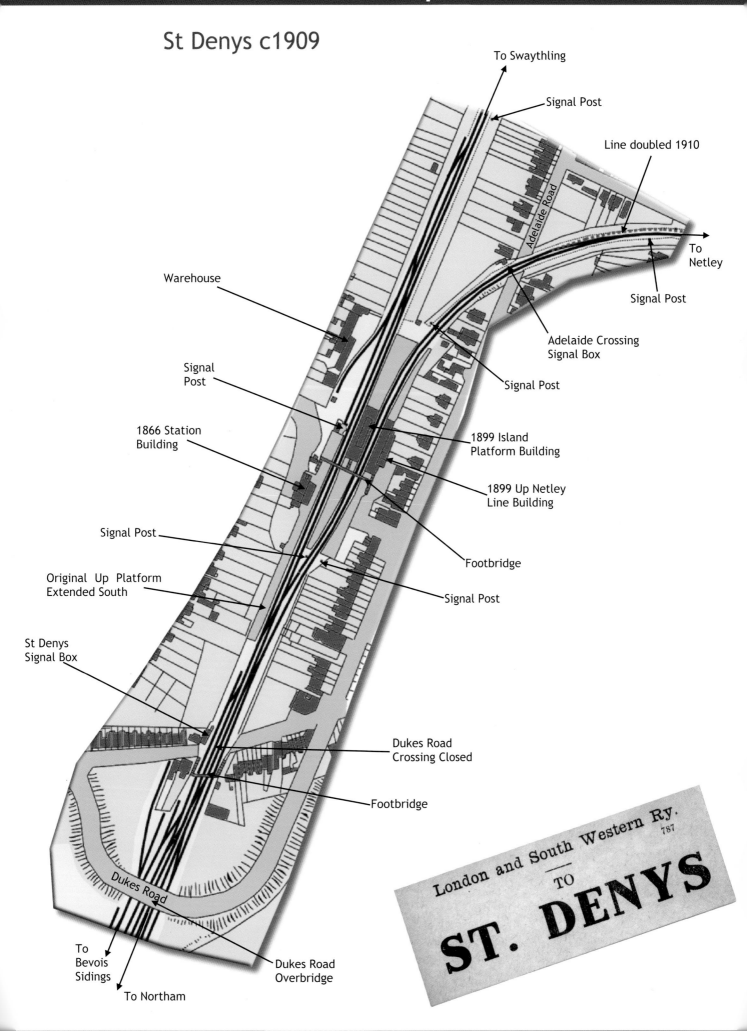

St Denys c1909

To Swaythling

Signal Post

Line doubled 1910

To Netley

Signal Post

Adelaide Crossing
Signal Box

Warehouse

Signal Post

Signal
Post

1899 Island
Platform Building

1866 Station
Building

1899 Up Netley
Line Building

Signal Post

Footbridge

Original Up Platform
Extended South

Signal Post

St Denys
Signal Box

Dukes Road
Crossing Closed

Footbridge

Dukes Road

To
Bevois
Sidings

Dukes Road
Overbridge

To Northam

London and South Western Ry.
787
TO
ST. DENYS

Left: M7 class No.30032 built in 1898 and withdrawn in July 1963 waits at the signals at St Denys on 23rd May 1953. The two signal posts were replaced by a gantry in 1955. Moving from left to right, the signals are the starter for down slow, and the distant for Mount Pleasant, starter for down fast and distant for Mount Pleasant. The two calling-on signals were to permit access to Bevois yard. These signals are identical for the down London line post.

(Photo: Ken Carr collection Copyright P. Fidczuk)

Right: A down parcels train with Ivatt class 2 2-6-2 tank locomotive No.41319, built at Crewe in 1952, in charge passes St Denys on 13th May 1965.
(Photo: P.Pescod Copyright transporttreasury.co.uk)

Left: Bulleid *West Country* Pacific *Blackmoor Vale* No.34023 steams into St Denys with a train from Bournemouth to Waterloo during the final days of steam. *Blackmoor Vale* was saved for preservation and today is based at the Bluebell Railway.
(Photographer Unknown)

Left: On 24th July 1960 *West Country* No. 34103 *Calstock* passes St Denys, the *Crawfords Cream Cracker* warehouse, served for many years by the railway, can be seen behind the engine.
(Photo: L.E. Elsey Copyright Colour-Rail 342880)

Right: Of course we all know that Southern Electrics can't run in snow, or maybe they can, as 4-CIG unit No.7352 pulls away from St Denys on 9th January 1982.
(Photo: R.Newman)

Left: A class 33 diesel pushing two EMU units on a down train having passed the disused signal gantry in the snow on 9th January 1982. Colour light signals controlled from Eastleigh had been introduced the previous October.
(Photo: R. Newman)

St Denys in the 1970s

Left: The magnificent station building at St Denys is seen from platform four on 27th April 1975. (Photo: R. Newman)

Right: The 1899 building on the rebuilt island platform at St Denys in 1974.

Below: When the station was rebuilt in 1899 a new platform and building were constructed for the up Netley line. They are seen here in 1974. The Solent Model Railway Group now occupies the building.

Right: Just to prove bus replacement services are nothing new, here are three *Hants and Dorset Lodekka* buses waiting in the yard on 3rd May 1975. These are in the red livery of the *National Bus Company*, as opposed to the 'true' *Hants and Dorset* green livery. Today where the photographer is standing is the new city centre link road. A new approach road has been built to the other end of the building. (Photo: R.Newman)

A Station Manager's Tale

Many of the photographs in this book come from the camera of Richard Newman, who was Station Manager at St Denys between 1974 and 1982. Here is his recollection of some of those days.

'I regard myself as very fortunate to have worked as Station Manager at St Denys. My previous appointment as a Southampton District relief clerk gave me a good grounding in booking, parcels and enquiry office work while latterly I had relieved the vacancy of Station Manager's clerk at Fareham, thereby gaining useful experience in staff and operating aspects.

Above: Winners of the *'Best Kept Station in S.W. Division'* competition in 1977 from left to right: Ken Chamberlain, Harold Street, Richard Newman, Ollie Davies, and Fred Eastman. (Photo: R.Newman collection)

Apart from the parent situation of St Denys, I was responsible for Swaythling (on the main) and Bitterne, Woolston and Sholing (on the Netley Branch) with a staff establishment of 29 including four booking clerks. Sholing was unstaffed so suffered occasional vandalism which had to be dealt with, while Swaythling saw a high volume of student traffic, particularly on Fridays, as it is near to the University.

On the main there was an hourly Waterloo-Bournemouth stopping service, worked by 4-VEP electric units, but the service had been halved when the Southampton to Alton via Alresford diesels ceased a couple of years earlier. Two trains an hour ran on the branch, one stopper, and one semi-fast Portsmouth to Salisbury extended to Bristol or Cardiff on alternate hours.

These were worked by the ultra reliable three car Hampshire (3H) DEMUs (with a couple retaining the original 2-car formation guaranteed to cause peak hour overcrowding). If for some reason they had been swopped from their booked working during the day, there was an occasional instance of running out of fuel on a late night service!

DEMUs ran to Bristol for a time, but proved unpopular with long distance passengers. The Western Region then contributed class 31 locos with sets of mark 1 carriages, while Diesel Mechanical Multiple Units (DMMUs) had also operated, but neither of them could keep time, thereby delaying other local services in the Southampton area. I remember a class 101 DMMU arrived at St Denys one day with a door hanging off as a girl on board had opened it in Southampton tunnel to get some air, whereupon it was struck by a passing train!

St Denys had a large signal box, continuously manned, on the junction. At Woolston the box was one-turn so it could be switched out at quieter times, making the section St Denys to Netley (or Fareham). Situated just beyond St Denys down branch platform was Adelaide Crossing, worked by three railwaymen. The gates had been replaced with full-width lifting barriers. Most signals were semaphore, including the impressive gantry at St Denys, and the oil lamps were attended to by the station foreman, Fred Eastman.

Many commercial duties were routine – collate the daily remittances from the outstations, combine with St Denys takings and prepare for the bank, which was about ¾ mile distant at Portswood. After an IRA incident in the area, which involved the local police chasing a suspect along the track, I was careful to vary my route!

Left: Ornamental brickwork above the booking office on the island platform in August 1982.

(Photo: R.Newman)

Left: Inside the booking office at St Denys with clerk Ken Chamberlain on 25th October 1982. Note the ticket racks, no computer printing here. (Photo: R.Newman)

offending goods vehicle always came off worse. On another occasion the Permanent Way gang unearthed a wartime incendiary device where Crawford's Biscuit siding had been and an Army Bomb Disposal Squad had to attend.

Winning the 'South West Division's Best Kept Station' competition was the greatest honour for St Denys. My staff made a real effort which even included a door-to-door leaflet drop to encourage new business, resulting in a first prize which attracted both press and regional TV coverage. During my years there we managed an increase of over 50% in tickets issued.

Wages retention was necessary as we paid out to staff of various departments through the booking office every Thursday. We would make up pay packets (and balance) on a Wednesday afternoon. There would then be visits to the outstations to check the accountancy (Station Managers had to use an orange crayon for this task) and, as time permitted, deal with correspondence arriving from the despatch bags from Waterloo, Wimbledon or Southampton and prepare staff duty rosters. Negotiation and consultation meetings had to be held with staff from time to time, while once a month the Southampton Area Manager (Cyril Earl) held a meeting with all station managers (Winchester, Eastleigh, St Denys, Southampton, Totton, Brockenhurst and Romsey) plus Yard Master and Motive Power Depot managers, Eastleigh and Freight Manager Bevois Park, to attend.

There were regular weekend engineering blocks in preparation for re-signalling, with the resultant replacement buses provided by Hants & Dorset. Ultimately the extension of the Eastleigh Panel box meant colour light signals replacing semaphores and the abolition of all manual signal boxes. An area reorganisation meant I was redundant in 1982 and with considerable sadness left 'the patch' for a temporary Instructor's post at the Eastleigh Traffic Training Centre.'

Richard Newman

I was lucky not to have an 'on-call', which was covered by Southampton, but I was usually phoned if something serious occurred by one of the three experienced St Denys signalmen, who could be relied upon to take initial action. I recall an incident one day when the 10.30 Waterloo to Weymouth divided between the 4-REP and TC units on the junction during a heavy snowstorm. Bridge strikes on the low bridge arch at Swaythling were not uncommon (as it was on the main A27), so trains had to be cautioned and the Bridge Inspector summoned. The

Above: Station foreman Fred Eastman *lamping* on 23rd February 1980.

Left: The station garden in August 1982, all now gone with the new link road. Note the poster with Jimmy Savile on the left. (Both Photos: R.Newman)

Swaythling

Above: A locomotive with an identity crisis. The photographer's description has this as *Merchant Navy* class No. 35008 *Orient Line* without name or number plates passing through Swaythling with the Newcastle to Poole through train on 15th April 1967. However, the chalked number on the buffer beam could also be No.35005 *Canadian Pacific* now preserved at the Mid-Hants Railway.
(Photo: John H.Bird Copyright SOUTHERN-images)

Beyond St Denys the quadruple track and marshalling yards are left behind as the railway passes through the suburbs of Southampton. While to the east of St Denys station housing was beginning to be developed, to the west much was still open parkland until the last decades of the nineteenth century. Having passed under St Denys road bridge, recently rebuilt to allow for larger containers to pass underneath, and past the site of the original Portswood station, the line is now on a half mile long embankment which Freeling's *Companion* states was twenty feet high climbing on a gradient of 1 in 469 stiffening to 1 in 400. In the 1870s this was still all farmland with the River Itchen on the right.

The railway now passes over the Kent Road overbridge, the approaches to which were widened in 1896-97 after the Corporation bought extra land from the LSWR. Further north a signal box existed at Woodmill from around the turn of the twentieth century until December 1930.

Freeling in his *Companion* then noted the 'pretty' river bridge at Woodmill, and, after passing under Woodmill Lane overbridge, he also noted South Stoneham House, originally built in 1708. At the time this was owned by the Fleming family, and later by a Captain Davison. Today it is a hall of residence for Southampton University.

Now the line curves into Swaythling station one and a half miles from St Denys. Freeling noted that the village of Swathling (the original name for Swaythling) lay down to

the east of the line, with a few houses and a mineral spring. He also stated that in 1839 it was intended to build a station near here but that the location had been 'not quite determined on'. It was to remain that way for another forty years.

Origins of Swaythling Station

The citizens of Swathling were obviously patient people. In February 1856 a request was made for a station, but nothing was done. However, in 1882, co-incidentally when the DN&SR were seeking powers for their line into Southampton with a station at Chilworth not far away, the LSWR sought to obtain Parliamentary powers to obtain a strip of land from Captain Davison in order to build a station. Davison successfully opposed the legislation in Parliament, but by February 1883 it was noted that the Company were constructing a station on their own land.

Swathling station opened on 15th October 1883. It consisted of a single-storey station building, built by

London and South Western Ry.
787
TO
SWAYTHLING

Above: An Edwardian scene at Swaythling as a train for the Town station enters the platform. It is worth noting that the coach body featured in the photo on page 11 has now been boarded over. Comparing this view with later photographs will show how little has changed at the station.
(Photo: Lens of Sutton Association)

J.Bull and Sons, connected to the down platform by a covered way, to allow for the possible quadrupling of the line. There were two platforms with timber waiting shelters and canopies, joined by a footbridge, which also replaced one built to preserve a right of way severed when the railway was built.

On the down side of the station was a small goods yard which had three sidings and a headshunt. Two of the sidings served a loading dock extended in the 1893-94. All this was controlled by a signal box built on the up side just south of the station.

Under the LSWR

In July 1895 the station was renamed Swaythling, and the following year a flight of steps was built from the road to the up platform. The LSWR obtained powers in 1900 to quadruple the line through the station. They authorised the work in May 1901, but in the October it was postponed because of financial considerations. This subsequently become indefinite. However, this does mean that Swaythling has remained the least changed of all the stations in Southampton.

World War One brought some changes to Swaythling with the addition of a new siding accessed from a new connection on the down line near Woodmill. This ran behind the goods yard to a loading dock and was used for loading horses in connection with the Army Remount Depot, being brought into use on 24th December 1914. It was taken out of use on 16th October 1923.

As already noted Southampton was the major embarkation port for troops during the war. On one day in April 1915 an observer at the station noted several trains from other railways passing through. These included two trains from the Great Eastern Railway, a GWR 4-4-0 tender locomotive on a London and North Western special, and an 'L' class 4-4-0 on a South Eastern and Chatham train.

The Southern

After World War One the rural character of Swaythling began to change as new estates were built on both sides of the line. Some of its busiest days though, probably came in 1932 when the Royal Agricultural Show was held at South Stoneham.

By the end of the 1930s war was looming once more, and in 1938 a test drill was performed near the station. It was imagined that a bomb had dropped on the bridge just north of the station causing a train wreck and fire.

This nearly became a reality on 19th January 1941 when a parachute bomb came through the roof of the booking office and crashed through the floor, sadly killing a dog as it did so. The ARP declared that the bomb had exploded and that staff could return to work. However, a little later the landlord of the *Masons' Arms* pub opposite came in and declared that it had not in fact gone off. Cue for a hasty evacuation before a bomb disposal team could deal with it. It was finally removed a fortnight later. The only other casualty of the war noted at Swaythling was of

Swaythling Station c1933

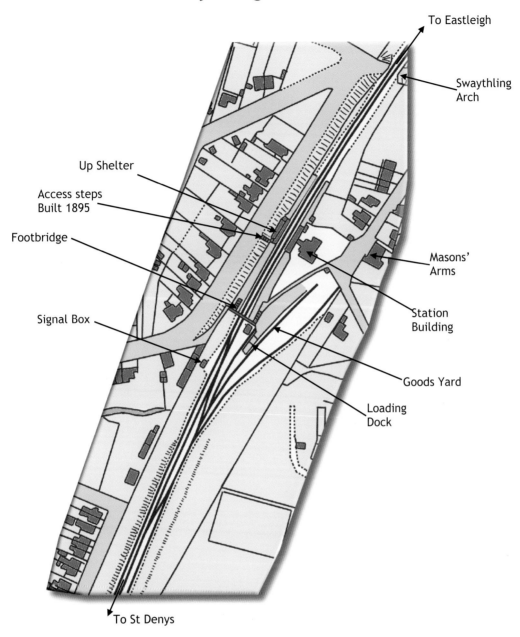

To Eastleigh

Swaythling Arch

Up Shelter

Access steps Built 1895

Footbridge

Masons' Arms

Signal Box

Station Building

Goods Yard

Loading Dock

To St Denys

signalman Seymour, who was killed on the line while walking to work at Eastleigh West box on 3rd March 1945.

British Railways

Staff at Swaythling clearly had pride in their station, even under British Railways, and in 1955 and 56 they won the 'Best Kept Station' award for class D stations in their area. However, gradually their station was to change. On 13th July 1959 the goods yard was closed and in October 1961 the sidings were removed.

With the advent of electrification Swaythling found itself at the northern end of one of the electrified sections. Conductor shoes tests for the new electric stock started

between Swaythling and Brockenhurst on 5th December 1966, and the current on the line to Lymington Junction was turned on, on 18th January 1967. In the meantime the introduction of colour light signalling led to the closure of Swaythling box on 6th November 1966. A new era was beginning.

Today the main station buildings at Swaythling look much as they did back when it was opened, and have been kept up very well. The goods yard has though been built over, and so housing now crowds the line on the east side. On the west side further road improvements took place in the 1980s. This can now be crossed on a new footbridge linked to the original station footbridge.

Right: *Battle of Britain* class No.34082 *615 Squadron,* built at Brighton in 1948 and rebuilt in 1960, passes Swaythling in March 1966. It was destined to be in service only a few more weeks, being withdrawn in April that year. The houses have now all been demolished.
(Photo: D.Wood Copyright R.K.Blencowe collection)

Left: On the other side of the footbridge another *Battle of Britain* No.34056 *Croydon* approaches Swaythling with an up train for Waterloo, passing Swaythling signal box in March 1966. This locomotive was destined to survive longer, being withdrawn in May 1967.
(Photo: D.Wood Copyright R.K.Blencowe collection)

Right: Swaythling signal box, seen here in March 1966, was another LSWR design of the 1880s. It is worth comparing with the photos of Chapel Crossing and Southampton Junction boxes of a similar period. The large roof ventilator is to be noted, a feature probably removed from the other boxes.
(Photo: D.Wood Copyright R.K.Blencowe collection)

Left: Controversial cargo, a nuclear flask train from Winfrith to Gloucester passes Swaythling on 25th October 1982 with class 33 No.33040 in charge.
(Photo: R. Newman)

Right: 4-TC Electric Multiple Unit No.431 at the rear of the 1.02pm Bournemouth to Waterloo passing through Swaythling on 25th October 1982.
(Photo: R.Newman)

Left: Swaythling station building in March 2011 looking little different from when it was built in 1883.

Right: Class 444 *Desiro* unit No.444022 passes Swaythling on 18th March 2011.

Southampton Airport

Above: *Merchant Navy* No.35013 *Blue Funnel* passes through the then recently-opened Southampton Airport station with a Waterloo bound train on 10th May 1966. Note the extensive use of concrete in the station's construction.

(Photo: L.E.Elsey Copyright Colour-Rail 341190)

Departing from Swaythling, just north of the station is the Swaythling underbridge, which has a very limited clearance. Over the years this has caught out many an unwary lorry or bus driver, with the result that their vehicle has become stuck fast underneath it. The author's father, who used this route to get to his teaching post, faced a long diversion on a number of occasions because of another driver ignoring the warning signs.

A train now crosses Monks Brook on an overbridge. Up until 30 years ago the land to the west of the line beyond this point was open countryside as the conurbation was left behind. However, now the new link road to the motorway runs alongside the line, while on the right hand side there is the *Ford Motor Co.* plant, first established in 1958, where Transit vans are manufactured. Now the M27 comes into view and a large overbridge crosses the line approximately a dozen lanes wide. Further on there used to be an occupation crossing known as Brown's crossing, but an agreement with the City Council in 1966 saw this taken out of use.

After this a train passes under Wide Lane bridge, which was built in 1907 to replace a level crossing and associated signal box constructed in 1881. It now enters the newest station in the Southampton area.

The origins of Southampton Airport (Parkway) station can

be traced back to the 1920s. What is now Southampton Airport was used for flying as far back as 1910, but during the First World War the United States Navy arrived in 1917 and constructed the original hangers. Following the war the site was used by a conglomeration of shipping companies to house migrants in transit to the United States from Eastern Europe, at a time when the government wished to control immigration.

It was then known as the *Atlantic Park Hostel* and when it opened in 1922 it could house up to 5,000 people. Many tens of thousands passed through the camp, but one unfortunate group of Ukrainian Jews ended up stuck at the camp for a number of years due to changes in immigration policy in the USA. They were cared for by charities and locals, and became part of the Eastleigh community.

Originally the migrants came to the camp via Eastleigh station, being transported to the hostel by road. However, on 30th October 1929 a halt was opened consisting of a single platform on the down line to permit direct transfers to take place, trains stopping at the halt by special arrangement.

This probably closed when the hostel was taken over by Southampton Council in 1932, and plans for an aerodrome were put forward. These included the possibility of a halt

Left: *Merchant Navy No.35028 Clan Line*, now preserved, approaches Wide Lane bridge with a train for Waterloo on 2nd July 1967. The *Ford Motor Co.* Factory can be seen in the background.
   (Photo: R.Cutler Copyright The Stephenson Locomotive Society)

being established on the railway, presumably an extension of the existing facility with a second platform, to allow direct access to the terminal. In the event the halt was not built, but the Southern was involved in the airport through its partnership in *Railway Air Services*, which began operating a service between London, Southampton and Cowes on 20th August 1934.

It was not until the electrification scheme was announced that a station at the Airport became a reality. On 1st April 1966 the station opened as Southampton Airport, and

originally had two 800ft long platforms, connected by a footbridge with a waiting room on the up platform.

In 1986 the station was upgraded with waiting shelters on both platforms, and with increased car parking facilities. It was then renamed Southampton Parkway for Southampton (Eastleigh) Airport on 29th September to encourage commuter traffic both to Southampton and London as well as serving the airport. There was another renaming on 29th May 1994 when it became Southampton Airport (Parkway).

Today nearly one and half million passengers use the station each year making it second only to Central in the Southampton area. During 2010 and into 2011 the station has been up-graded again with a new footbridge with lifts and a multi-storey car park.

Plan of Atlantic Park Halt c1931

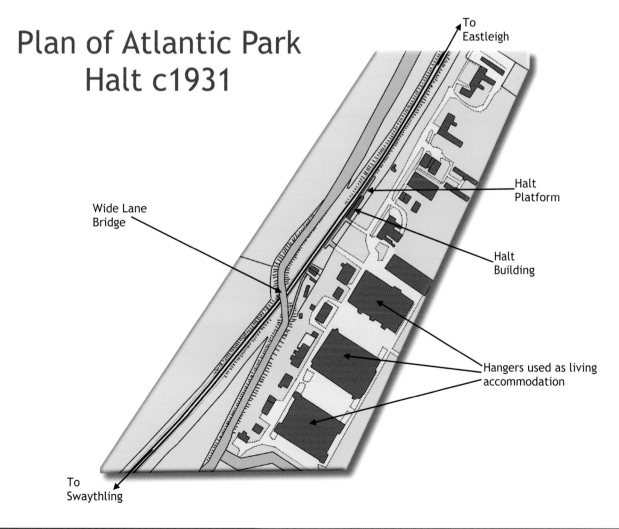

To Eastleigh

Halt Platform

Wide Lane Bridge

Halt Building

Hangers used as living accommodation

To Swaythling

Right: On 5th March 1994 4-CIG unit No.1311 in *Network South East* livery pulls into Southampton Parkway. Headcode 93 denoted a slow train from Waterloo to Bournemouth.
(Photographer Unknown)

Left: Class 444 *Desiro* unit No.444014 pulls into Southampton Airport (Parkway) on 19th March 2011, with a train for Waterloo. The original concrete footbridge still remains, but now a modern footbridge with lifts has also been provided.

Below: The station building at Southampton Airport (Parkway) on 19th March 2011, with building work taking place in connection with a new multi-storey car park.

The Southampton & Dorchester Railway

Above: The lack of any signal box west of the level crossing points to this being a pre-1872 view of Southampton West station taken from above the tunnel entrance. Items of interest include the large circular disc signal seen over the top of the down shelter. There are also locking bars over the rails on the sidings, and also the 'enclosure' at the end of the up-siding, possibly indicating a private loading area. The closest house on the right is *Alessandro House*, later the residence of the stationmaster. Note the affluent 'villas' on the right compared with the terraced housing on the left. In the foreground there are piles of sleepers, while the water laps the shoreline in the distance. (Photo: Cope collection, University of Southampton)

The origins of the Southampton and Dorchester Railway were dealt with earlier in this volume, and a more complete history of the line will feature in *Southern Rails Around Bournemouth*. However, very few railways can have had such a dramatic run-up to its opening day, which ended up being a somewhat anti-climatic affair. Part of the drama surrounded Southampton tunnel.

This tunnel had been a source of contention from the beginning, as the railway's original preferred route to the Royal Pier had been vetoed by the Harbour Commissioners. Now there were discussions with the Council about the length of the tunnel, with the Corporation insisting that it should be longer than the S&DR wished in order to preserve parkland.

In the end the tunnel was constructed by conventional tunnelling under the almshouses, situated just east of the site of Blechynden station, and then by the 'cut and cover' method for the rest of its 528 yard length. However, part of this passed over the former Salisbury and Southampton Canal tunnel, and this combined with the geology of the area caused issues.

However, in January 1847 the tunnelling undermined the foundations of the almshouses causing them to subside, and so they had to be demolished. Then on 2nd May 1847 a ten yard section of the tunnel collapsed under London

Road. Two pedestrians on the road fell into the tunnel below, but amazingly walked out of the eastern portal unscathed!

Finally the tunnel passed its inspection, but the 110 yard radius curve that connected the line to the London line at Southampton Junction was said by the Inspector to offer an 'example to be avoided' because of the sharp radius. The LSWR later eased it to a 198 yard radius. The line's opening was set for 1st June 1847, but on Sunday 30th May problems were noted in the tunnel.

These had arisen where the railway crossed the old canal tunnel, here the contractors had tried to stabilise the old tunnel, but had prevented the drainage of water from it. This led to a build up of water which undermined the railway tunnel, and made more repairs necessary.

Meanwhile, the previous Saturday, the 29th May, a special meeting of the Southampton Town Council Dorchester Railway Committee had resolved to obtain an injunction to prevent the railway from opening. This was because of the lack of a station at Blechynden as required by the Act of Parliament, the reasons for which will be given later. The opening was under threat from two fronts.

Two directors of the S&DR sought to re-assure the Council about the station, by immediately taking a two-year lease

Above: Adams class T6 4-4-0 No.680 arrives at Southampton West with a Bournemouth Express at the turn of the century. At the up platform is what appears to be a MSWJR train presumably on its way to the Town station. Only having two through platforms for the number of trains passing through it meant that stopping times were short and swift departures demanded smart work from train and station staff. (Photo: Lens of Sutton Association)

on *Ivy House* near the railway at Blechynden, to be used as a temporary station until a permanent one could be built. They took possession on the Monday morning, 31st May. However, by then it was clear the tunnel was not going to be ready. Workers were unwilling to work in the tunnel, even when enhanced wages were offered, such was their concern. Notices were printed stating that the opening was postponed.

However, it was eventually decided to still open the line on the 1st June, but only from the temporary station at Blechynden. This meant locomotives and carriages had to be transported through the streets of Southampton from the terminus station by teams of horses, which must have been quite a sight.

Finally, two trains departed for Dorchester on the 1st June, with one making the return journey. The *Hampshire Advertiser* reported that passenger numbers were less than expected due to the confusion about whether the opening would happen or not. However, trade seems to have soon built up.

Early Developments

The lack of facilities at Blechynden hampered operations, and presumably at least one locomotive had to be stored in the open overnight. A basic train service of five trains in each direction started on Monday 7th June 1847 utilising two train sets. It also needs to be remembered that when opened the S&DR was, save for the double

track between Southampton and Redbridge, the longest single track line in the country.

Services were finally able to run through the tunnel from 5th August 1847, and so trains could now run to and from the terminus station. Still the same basic service remained, but now goods trains were also run. Initially there was no electric telegraph, trains simply crossing on the basis of the timetable. But following a collision near Wareham, the new system was in place by the end of 1847.

On 20th January 1857 services were extended to Weymouth running over GWR rails from Dorchester, and now consisted of seven up (two of which were mixed), and six down trains on weekdays. Further expansion of services also resulted from the doubling of the lines between Redbridge and Beaulieu Road on 1st August 1858, with doubling being completed as far as Wimborne by the end of the September.

Other lines were now connected to the original S&DR. In 1851 the Eling Tramway was opened, and on 12th July 1858 the Lymington branch commenced operation.

Another major change came when the Northam curve came into operation on 2nd August 1858, enabling direct Waterloo to Bournemouth trains to be run. At the same time Blechynden was re-named Southampton West.

Around this time too there had been several schemes in relationship to the route from Redbridge to Romsey, some

Route from Northam to Totton
Based on 1945 Ordnance Survey Map

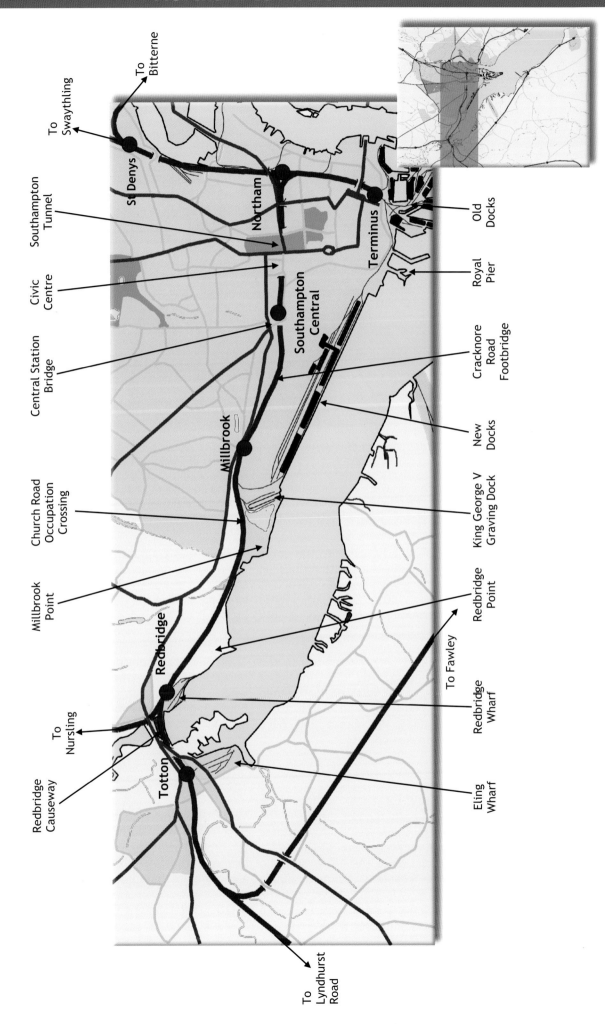

To Bitterne

To Swaythling

St Denys

Southampton Tunnel

Northam

Civic Centre

Terminus

Old Docks

Royal Pier

Central Station Bridge

Southampton Central

Cracknore Road Footbridge

Church Road Occupation Crossing

Millbrook

New Docks

King George V Graving Dock

Millbrook Point

Redbridge

Redbridge Point

To Fawley

Redbridge Causeway

To Nursling

Totton

Redbridge Wharf

Eling Wharf

To Lyndhurst Road

Above: There is much to see in this photo of *King Arthur* class 4-6-0 No.741 *Joyous Gard,* built in 1919, passing the remains of the old (pre-1895) Southampton West station probably c1925. Note the number of trucks on the sidings to the left, while beyond them, the light coloured house is *Alessandro House,* the stationmaster's residence. In the centre is the entrance to Southampton tunnel, while to the right is housing, some of which was demolished to allow the building of Civic Centre Road. In front of the houses the gate through which the line to the power station passed can be observed, while on the extreme right can be seen some buffer stops to sidings laid in connection with the train ferries by Royal Pier during World War One.

(Photo: S.Braggington collection Kidderminster Railway Museum)

of which involved either making a new line to the docks or obtaining running powers along the existing lines. In part to counter these moves a new station was opened at Millbrook on 1st November 1861. Eventually these proposals resulted in the opening of the A&RR on 6th March 1865.

The growth of the area around Christchurch led to the opening of the line from Ringwood on 13th November 1862. This was then extended to the outskirts of, the then rapidly developing, Bournemouth on 14th March 1870. Eventually on 5th March 1888 the direct line from Brockenhurst to Bournemouth was opened.

Trains

During the 19th century the passenger rolling stock changed considerably. In the early days of the S&DR the carriages were still inspired by the stage coach, but later other four-wheeled designs evolved. Then in the 1870s six-wheel coaches appeared, while the 1880s saw the first appearance of bogie coaches. *Pullman* dining coaches, as already mentioned, were introduced onto the route from 1890, while corridor stock was not seen working regularly on the Bournemouth line until the 1910s.

Among the first locomotives to be seen on the S&DR were two of the original 2-2-2 tender locomotives of the LSWR, Nos. 23 and 24 *Antelope* and *Reindeer.* Of course longer and heavier trains demanded more powerful locomotives,

so later four-coupled locomotives appeared, first of the 2-4-0 tender design favoured by Joseph Beattie, and then the 4-4-0s of Adams and Drummond designs. Goods trains were handled in the latter days of the nineteenth century by 0-6-0 tender locomotives, while 0-4-4 tanks handled local passenger services.

Train services continued to develop along the line, particularly during the early years of the 20th century when new express services were introduced from Bournemouth to destinations in the north, and also to Brighton. By 1909 33 passenger trains, ten goods trains and a horsebox train passed through Southampton West in the down direction every weekday.

The First World War

Major troop movements occurred at the outbreak of the First World War, with soldiers heading for Southampton for embarkation to France. Many of these came from camps in the New Forest, and so troop trains were run along the Southampton & Dorchester into the docks.

A later development was the provision of a Train Ferry terminal to the west of the Royal Pier, which was connected to the mainline near Southampton West. However, this was short-lived with services to Dieppe starting on 13th December 1917, and only lasting until the early months of 1919. The story of the train ferries will be dealt with in *Southern Rails on Southampton Docks.*

Below: Part of a legal notice from Sir John Barker Mill for compensation from the S&DR for building across part of his property along the shore at Millbrook and Eling.

To the Southampton and Dorchester Railway Company

Take Notice that Sir John Barker Mill of Mottisfont Abbey in the County of Southampton Baronet is interested in certain lands part of which you are empowered by the Southampton and Dorchester Railway Act one thousand eight hundred and forty five to take and use for the said Railway that is to say certain Shore and Mudlands situate in the Parishes of Millbrook and Eling in the said County of Southampton delineated on the Map annexed to this Notice and therein colored pink and that the said Sir John Barker Mill is interested therein as the Tenant for life with remainder to the use of his Children as Tenants in common in tail with remainder to the use of the said Sir John Barker Mill as the Heir of his late Uncle Sir Charles Mill Baronet deceased in fee and he hereby as well for himself and his Heirs as for all other parties interested therein in remainder reversion or expectancy claims compensation for damages sustained or which will be sustained by him or them by reason of the severing of the part of the said Shore and Mudland above the Line of Railway from the residue thereof below the said line and by reason of severing the land so taken, or to be taken, by you for the construction of the said Railway from the rest of the Shore and Mudland belonging to the said Sir John Barker Mill and also for damage and deterioration in value of the residue of the said Shore and Mudland by the Construction of the said Railway and execution of the works thereof whereby the residue of the shore and Mudland of the said Sir John Barker Mill has been or will be injuriously affected And take Notice that the amount of compensation for the several matters hereinbefore referred to claimed by the said Sir John Barker Mill Baronet is Three thousand Eight hundred and thirty pounds and that unless the said sum shall be paid or duly deposited by you in the Bank of England under the provisions of the said Act and of the Lands clauses Consolidation Act one thousand eight hundred and forty five within twenty one days after the receipt of this Notice it is the desire of the said Sir John Barker Mill Baronet that the amount of Compensation due to him in

Above: *Merchant Navy* No.35027 *Port Line* is in charge of the *Bournemouth Belle* as it crosses Redbridge Causeway on 5th May 1959. *Port Line* was preserved and is currently being overhauled.
(Photo: G.F.Bloxam)

Grouping

During the days of the Southern the fortunes of the former S&DR around Southampton were dominated by a number of factors. First came the opening of the Totton, Marchwood and Fawley Light Railway in July 1925, which will be documented later.

Next came the New (or Western) Docks project, which involved the reclamation of 400 acres of land, much of which was alongside the line between Southampton West and Millbrook. Sidings were put in between Southampton West and Millbrook in 1927 to allow access for construction trains to the works. Then in 1935 connections into the New Docks were made just west of Millbrook.

This was part of the work which led to the re-construction and enlargement of Southampton West, during which it was re-named Southampton Central, together with the quadrupling of the line between Central and Millbrook, and the re-building of Millbrook station. All of these came into use in 1935. Before this new trains were introduced, the *Bournemouth Limited* in 1929 and the *Bournemouth Belle* from 1931, which have already been mentioned.

The Second World War

The New Docks meant that on the outbreak of the Second World War the former S&DR in Southampton handled a

significant number of the troop trains as soldiers of the Expeditionary Force headed for France. There was considerable traffic as well from the evacuation at Dunkirk. However, the heaviest usage came with the D-Day landings, and the rapid movement of troops and equipment from holding camps throughout Hampshire and Dorset to take part in the biggest sea landing in history. To facilitate access to the New Docks, a junction was built between Redbridge and Millbrook in 1943 to allow trains from Bournemouth and from the Salisbury line, to run directly into the docks.

At the outbreak of war there was a significant evacuation of children and adults from Southampton to the New Forest, and other less 'at risk' areas. This led to the running of many special services to cater for this process. Further traffic on the line was generated by the military port at Marchwood which commenced operations in 1943, with a rail connection to the Fawley branch.

During the war too the line suffered from bombing with at least three major instances of bomb damage. One closed the line east of Southampton tunnel at Six Dials for a number of days, with trains to and from Bournemouth being re-routed through the Old and New Docks from Southampton Terminus, or via Romsey and Chandlers Ford. Southampton Central was attacked several times, two of which resulted in a lot of destruction. In addition there was also damage to the works at Redbridge, and also Eling Wharf.

Above: *Hymek* diesel No. D7035 passes Millbrook with the 9.40am Birmingham New Street to Poole on 6th May 1967.
(Photo: John H. Bird Copyright SOUTHERN-images)

Following the War and Nationalisation

Fairly quickly after the war train services on the former S&DR began to pick up. The *Bournemouth Belle* was re-introduced in 1946, and passenger numbers started to climb. In many senses Nationalisation had little effect on the line initially. There was the interest of the 1948 locomotive exchanges, and the gradual introduction of new locomotive types. Some early mainline diesels were seen in operation in the 1950s, but steam generally held sway through to the 1960s. By 1964 the basic hourly service between Southampton and Bournemouth consisted of one non-stop or semi-fast, and one slow, with occasional trains to Fawley, Lymington and Ringwood. However, the axe was about to fall.

One casualty during the days of the Southern was the line from Ringwood to Christchurch via Hurn, closed in September 1935. Now further closures came. On 2nd May 1964 the last passenger services ran on the section of the former S&DR between Brockenhurst and Bournemouth via Ringwood and Wimborne. The track between Brockenhurst and Ringwood was lifted in 1966, and the same year passenger services were withdrawn from the Fawley branch.

Electrification and Privatisation

However, by now electrification was on the cards through Southampton to Bournemouth. By December 1966 tests were being carried out on the new conductor rail as far as Brockenhurst, with the current being turned on from 18th January 1967. The full electric service was introduced from Monday 10th July 1967, steam having been withdrawn the day before. At Southampton Central the old up side buildings were demolished, and replaced with an office block, the station being renamed Southampton. Freight traffic patterns were also changing. The decline of the mixed goods train and the handing of coal at stations led to the closure of goods yards along the line. However, at Southampton a new form of goods traffic was emerging, the container. This was pioneered by the LSWR in the nineteenth century when meat was packed into carts at Southampton docks then loaded on wagons, so that they could be rolled off in London and delivered. In the 1960s containerisation of sea-transported goods took off in a major way. At Millbrook in 1968 the first *Freightliner* container terminal opened, with the Maritime Container Port opening in 1972.

By the late 1970s Monday to Friday passenger services consisted of hourly fast, semi-fast and slow services between Southampton and Bournemouth. These were supplemented by through services between Weymouth and Leeds, Birmingham, Liverpool, Manchester and Bradford, and services between Poole and Newcastle, Nottingham, Sheffield and Birmingham.

In 1981 the lines between Northam Junction and Millbrook were converted for reversible running, and in 1988 class 442 *Wessex* units made their appearance. *Stagecoach* took over the running of many of the electric services on the line in 1996 under the name *South West Trains*, and the through trains to the north are handled by *Cross Country*. Latterly *South West Trains* services have made use of *Desiro* units, while *Cross Country* trains consist of diesel-electric *Voyagers*. One interesting service that uses the line between Northam Junction and Redbridge is the *South West Trains* hourly circular that runs in each direction between Salisbury, Romsey, Redbridge, Millbrook, Southampton, Eastleigh, Chandlers Ford, and Romsey again.

Southampton Central

Above: *Battle of Britain* class No.34056 *Croydon* arrives at Southampton Central with the 11.30am from Waterloo to Bournemouth on 28th March 1967. Note the conductor rails are in place for electrification, and the footbridge is being painted, although with an interesting approach to Health and Safety. (Photo: P.F.Bloxam)

Origins

It seems incredible today, seeing the hive of activity at Southampton Central station that it was very nearly not built. When originally conceived the architects of the Southampton and Dorchester had in mind a line running to the Royal Pier in Southampton, and then linked by a tramway to the LSWR's Southampton station. Their plans were changed because of the refusal of the Harbour Commissioners to permit steam engines to be used on the tramway, to an inland route via Northam to the LSWR station. Initially there were no plans for another station around Southampton save for the one planned at Redbridge.

But after representations from the Council a clause was inserted in the Bill in committee in May 1845 that required the building of a station near Blechynden Terrace. This was at a site known as King John's Pond, and to arrange for 'ample' trains to stop there. In part it was a recognition that the there needed to be a station nearer the town centre than the LSWR terminus. It also served the new suburbs that were springing up around the area.

However, construction was not to prove straightforward. There were discussions on whether the main buildings should be on the north or south side of the line, the north favouring the new suburbs, the south the town centre,

and also on who was responsible for the construction of the approach roads.

Then there was litigation, a dispute arose with the tenant of the site at King John's Pond over a strip of land it was claimed the Company had taken illegally. This led to the tenant serving an injunction on the S&DR in April 1847 to prevent them proceeding with building the station until the matter was settled. In addition, on 22nd May 1847, a case was brought that the S&DR had broken promises to the owner of *Kingsbridge House* about the siting of the station, and again an injunction was sought to prevent opening.

All this was the prelude to the events of the weekend preceding the opening reported earlier. The Town Council, faced with the proposition that the S&DR would open without a station at Blechynden, decided to seek their own injunction, at which point the leasing of *Ivy House* as a temporary station building saved the day.

Should the Council have been concerned? On the one hand at the court case on the 22nd it was stated that a platform had already been erected at the site, which seems to indicate that the railway was trying to fulfil its obligations. However, later in the year when the line was fully open there were complaints that only two trains a day were stopping there. This led to the LSWR having to

Above: *King Arthur* class No.30449 *Sir Torre* traverses Southampton Junction with a train for Southampton Terminus from Salisbury.
(Photo: B.Moody Collection)

give an undertaking to the Council at the beginning of 1848 that all trains would stop there. Therefore, perhaps the Company was ambivalent about the station. However, by forcing the Company to rent *Ivy House* the Council probably did the railway a favour by giving them a base from which to operate trains on opening day after the tunnel collapsed.

From Southampton Junction to Central

To gain access to the station trains left the original LSWR line at Southampton Junction on the curve previously mentioned. When Northam curve was built, the two lines met to form a triangle at Tunnel Junction. Here was one of the of the oldest signal boxes on the railway, possibly dating from 1858, which existed until being taken out

of service in October 1966 and later demolished.

Now the tracks run in a cutting behind a row of shops on Northam Road, before passing under the St Mary's Road overbridge. Just to the north of the line here on 8th July 1941, a bomb fell demolishing the adjoining property, debris from which blocked the line, and trains had to be diverted for a number of days.

The line continued to run along the backs of the houses and past Trinity church, all now gone, until plunging into Southampton tunnel. It was here on 23rd June 1888 a

Right: A view of Tunnel Junction signal box from the approaching *Eastleigh Venturer* special on 11th November 1962.
(Photo: F.C.Hammersley)

Above: Bomb damage at the St Mary's Street bridge on 8th July 1941. The line had to be closed to clear the debris and through trains were either routed through the docks and Town Quay or via Romsey and Eastleigh.   (Photo: R.K.Blencowe collection)

Below: On 6th August 1983 repairs to Southampton tunnel are going on resulting in single line working being imposed, and so 4-REP No.3009 emerges 'wrong-line' from the eastern portal of the tunnel at the head of a Waterloo semi-fast.

(Photo: E.W.Fry Copyright R.K. Blencowe collection)

Above: LSWR T14 class 4-6-0 No.462 departs Southampton West through the remains of the old (pre-1895) Southampton West station sometime after 1917, when the loco was superheated.

(Photo: S.Braggington collection Copyright Kidderminster Railway Museum)

passenger train from Brockenhurst to Southampton Docks station collided with the back of a goods train from Weymouth to Bishopstoke, which was standing at Tunnel Junction at approximately 6.44pm. The main cause was that the passenger train had departed from Southampton West without checking the starting signal was 'off'. However, the distant signal for Tunnel Junction, which was at the eastern portal of the tunnel, was only visible when the tunnel was clear of steam. It was therefore recommended that a repeater for the distant signal was added at the western end of the tunnel.

Having passed through the 528 yard long tunnel, which

takes the line under the City Centre parks and the Civic Centre, trains emerged alongside Kingsbridge Lane on the right, now just a pedestrian path. Here also stood *Alessandro House*, which was purchased for the use of stationmasters in 1887. Further up the bank on the right was Kingsbridge House, part of the grounds of which housed King Edward VI School until its move to its present site in the 1930s. On the left of the line was the site of King John's Pond.

Running into Blechynden station the train was now parallel to Blechynden Terrace and the new approach road from the Town Centre, which ran along the shoreline

Right: *Merchant Navy* No.35018 *British India Line* is seen in the experimental British Railways express blue livery departing from Central past the site of the pre-1895 station in October 1949. This was the first of the *Merchant Navy* class to be re-built in 1956, and has been preserved.

(Photo: W.E.Robertson Copyright Colour-Rail BRS913)

SOUTHAMPTON WEST

"JACK" THE RAILWAY DOG.

Left: The LSWR Railway Servants' Orphanage at Woking was opened in 1909, having been established in Clapham by Revd Canon Allen Edwards in 1885. To raise funds for the Orphanage various means were used, and at Southampton West "Jack" (there were a number of them) the railway dog had a distinguished career raising funds by means of the collecting box strapped to his back as seen in the picture. Later a stuffed "Jack", who used to work in London, was used at Southampton West from 1916. He remained there until 1966, and is still remembered by the author.
(Commercial Postcard)

on the left. It now enters the station which was for many years a very simple affair.

From Blechynden to West

The original temporary arrangement seems to have lasted for three years, until a more permanent structure was in use in 1850. The main building was, it was rumoured, originally destined for Cosham before being erected on the north, or up side, of the line. It was a simple timber affair with a 60ft platform, and was staffed at this point by three people.

A new era came when the Northam curve was opened, and the station was renamed Southampton West, or West End, from 2nd August 1858. However, the station continued to be known by all three names until at least the end of the nineteenth century! It was reported that the new arrangements were to make 'the Blechynden station the principal one for departure from, and arrival at, Southampton'. Possibly slightly over-optimistic at the time, as most trains still went to, or originated from, the Docks station.

In October 1859 approval was given for a new enlarged station, completed in late 1860 by J.Bull and Sons. On the up side there was a building with a booking office, two waiting rooms and from 1862, a canopy, while on the down side there was a shelter with two waiting rooms. To the east of the station there were short sidings on the up and down side added by 1870, and to the west the level crossing connecting Blechynden Street to the new Western Esplanade road. Here new crossing gates and a signal box were provided in 1872, while another goods siding was added on the up side in 1871.

It is difficult today to appreciate that up until the building

of the power station in the 1900s, that the station lay right on the shoreline. This is due to the amount of land that was reclaimed for the New Docks in the 1930s. However, its position meant that the station was subject to frequent flooding and storm damage during the 19th century.

A New Station

However, the facilities at the new station rapidly started to become inadequate. The platforms were lengthened in 1865, 1870 and 1887, but thoughts soon turned to the provision of an entirely new station. Land was purchased from the Corporation and building work commenced in 1894 on the site to the west of the Blechynden Street crossing, which had been considered for closure since 1884.

On 1st November 1895 the new station was opened. Its construction had been a large undertaking with 30ft deep foundations being built in the mud with concrete supporting arches. The station still only had two through platforms the up side being 600ft long and the down 800ft, with a 500ft bay road on the down side. On the up side was an ornate new set of buildings in the Flemish Queen Anne style, with an 82ft high clock tower. Meanwhile on the down side, another substantial brick building was constructed, with a covered footbridge connecting both platforms at the eastern end of the station.

At the same time the goods yard had been extended on the up side, and there was another siding off the down bay. In addition, the old station building had been retained as a goods shed, and the old level crossing remained, although a footbridge had been built across it in 1885. Next to the crossing a signal box was provided

Right: A view of the up side of Southampton West taken between 1904 when the power station was constructed on reclaimed land on the down side of the station, and 1913 when the Divisional Office was opened at the near end of the forecourt. The Queen Anne style of the building and iconic clock-tower can be clearly seen.
(Photo: Lens of Sutton Association)

Left: This posed view has workers almost everywhere, up the telegraph pole, and working on the roof of the down building. Note the gates to the entrance of the down forecourt, as well as the ornate footbridge, and the level crossing behind the 'sweepers'.
(Photo: Lens of Sutton Association)

Right: A close up view of the signal box by the crossing on this postcard of '445' class 4-4-0 No.453 in the up platform. The train could possibly be a through working to Birmingham composed of GWR stock.
(Commercial Postcard)

Left: On 4th August 1926 *King Arthur* class No.777 *Sir Lamiel* stands at the end of the up platform at Southampton West. The decorated panels on the footbridge are worthy of note. No.777 was part of a batch of 30 locomotives built in 1925 by the North British Locomotive Co., and known as the *Scotch Arthurs*. It is now preserved as part of the National Collection.
(Photo: Copyright Kidderminster Railway Museum)

Above: Never believe all you see as another *Scotch Arthur* No.784 *Sir Nerovens* stands in the down platform at Southampton West with a Bournemouth train on 4th August 1926. Note the West ground frame building on the left, while on the right a train stands in the bay platform. However, interestingly this photo is a composite of two pictures, look the base of the nearest lamppost and the legs of the man on the right, so it might not be quite as it seems! (Photo: Copyright Kidderminster Railway Museum)

with a 24-lever frame, although there is a question as to whether this was a new box or a re-build, as well as ground frames at each end of the station. Now the station did begin to take on the air of the main station in Southampton.

Into the 20th Century

Over the course of the next few years traffic began to develop substantially, with through services being introduced to different parts of the country, which have been described on page 72. In 1904 the Corporation power station was opened on re-claimed land south of the down line between the tunnel and the old station. A connection was laid across the Western Esplanade road from the down side for coal wagons to be transferred to the station by the Corporation's own electric locomotives.

Further developments followed. 1905 saw additional awnings being provided on the down side, while in 1906 the down side building of the old station was demolished leaving just a canopy. The down platform and bay were lengthened by 100ft, along with other alterations to the track layout. A new office building for the Divisional Manager was also built outside the up building in 1912-13.

The First World War

Mr. Thorton Burge took charge of Southampton West as stationmaster in 1914, it was to be a busy time for him and his staff. During the First World War it is estimated that three million passengers, 97,000 parcels, 51,000 milk churns, 100,000 telegrams and 25,000 tons of coal passed through the station annually. As well as of course all the extra trains that were run at various times.

To cater for the troops using the station, particularly those returning from the Front, the Young Men's Christian

Above: The new footbridge under construction at Southampton Central, taken from the approach road to the new road overbridge. The old down platform is being rebuilt as an island platform, and a new down platform is being constructed nearest the camera. On the extreme right the foundations for the new down buildings can be seen.   (Photo: R.K.Blencowe Collection)

Right: The scene from approximately the same spot in January 2011.

Association (YMCA) built a hut at the eastern end of the up station yard, to provide catering and recreational facilities. This was manned by the station staff and their families on a voluntary basis. Another development saw a connection laid from the down bay road to the Train Ferry pier near the Royal Pier in 1917.

From West to Central

After the war things began to return to normal, but the station remained busy. Out in the station yard the former YMCA hut was taken over by the railway and the Docks and Marine Social Club opened. Then in 1923 the station came under the auspices of the Southern.

In 1926 the Divisional Office was extended, and a parcels office and cloakroom erected. Then in 1927 the up platform was extended westwards by 300ft and the west end ground frame moved. However, traffic continued to grow and it soon became clear that extra facilities were needed, not least because of the proposed development of the New Docks.

Therefore, the quadrupling of the lines between Southampton West and Millbrook was suggested, with both West and Millbrook stations being rebuilt. Facilities at West would be increased with two more platform roads, and also the level crossing would be replaced with a 170ft long, 40ft wide, overbridge across the western

end of the platforms. Work started in 1933 with the contract for the overbridge being let to R.McAlpine and Sons.

Tragedy, however, had twice struck at the station with the loss of two stationmasters. On 20th June 1932 Mr. A.J.Hardy passed away, and just over a year later on 22nd September 1933 his successor Mr. F.J.Radford died at the age of 54. This must have been an unsettling time for the staff.

Happily there were better occasions to celebrate, such as the presentation to goods porter Andrews to mark his marriage in 1936. While the staff was very male dominated women did work at the station such as Mrs. Hoskins. She retired as a waiting room attendant in October 1937, being presented with a handbag and bouquet.

Meanwhile the new station had opened in 1935 with four 900ft through platforms, and a 470ft bay road on the down side. On the up side the old 1895 buildings had been retained, while the down platform was converted to an island platform, with a new down platform being built, and the old down building demolished. In its place a new *Odeon*-style booking hall was constructed with associated offices, and refreshment room, parcels office etc. In the booking hall there was also a map showing the positions of the ships in the docks.

Left: Adams designed 0-4-2 A12 *Jubilee* class No.609 waits in the bay platform five at Central in 1939 with a train for Fawley.

(Photo: J.W.Neve)

Royalty also frequented the station. Among the recorded occasions was when Princess Beatrice travelled to Weymouth and back from the station in 1902. On 8th November 1932 the Duke and Duchess of York made use of the station on a visit to open the first stage of the new Southampton Civic Centre that had been built on land over the tunnel. They also visited the New Docks to view progress on construction. As will be seen, a few years later the Duke would return as King in less happy circumstances. The completion of the Civic Centre project was also marked by a Royal visit, this time by the Duke and Duchess of Gloucester, who arrived on the *Bournemouth Belle* on 26th April 1939.

Connecting the platforms was a new covered footbridge, while the old level crossing bridge had been extended across the four tracks to preserve the pedestrian right of way. At the west end of the up platform a new signal box was built with an A2 75 lever *Westinghouse* frame. The new facilities were all in use by 7th July 1935 when the station was renamed Southampton Central. Sadly not all of them were to survive long.

Traffic

It is worth taking a moment at this point to reflect on some of the different types of special traffic that the station handled. Amongst these were the theatre trains, which ran both in connection with the *Empire,* now *Mayflower,* theatre nearby, and also to take people to London for shows at the *Palladium.* The presence of the Southampton Football Club's ground, The Dell, in the vicinity, was another source of special traffic on match days, including of course taking Southampton fans to away fixtures. In January 1938, for example, 700 supporters travelled to Birmingham for the match with Aston Villa.

There were other events too. Exhibition trains frequently visited the station. In December 1934 it was said that 5,800 visitors frequented the train of *J.S.Fry & Son,* makers of sweets and chocolates, so one can guess at the attraction!

One new innovation was the installation of loudspeakers in August 1936 to assist passengers find their trains. In 1937 the Docks and Marine Sports Club, was enlarged, with new facilities, including a miniature rifle range, being opened on 11th December. Another happy occasion that year was the week of 17th-24th July when the station was decorated for Merchant Navy Week, with a special exhibition in one of the sheds at the New Docks. However, by now the war clouds were beginning to gather.

Right: Drummond designed L11 class 4-4-0 No.157 with a train of GWR stock, including two clerestory coaches, on a Wolverhampton to Bournemouth working in 1939. While waiting the fireman is taking the chance to 'step out' for some cleaning. No.157 was converted to oil firing for a few months in 1947-48 before being laid aside and finally withdrawn in 1952.

(Photo: J.W.Neve)

World War Two

There is a picture of sandbags outside Southampton Central in preparation for air-raids taken in November 1938, so plans were being made well in advance of the day war actually broke out. Among these was the development of a concrete bunker to act as the District Control Room, which was built on the up side near the tunnel mouth. It was said to have had walls up to 5ft thick, and is now the site of the telephone exchange.

Amazingly the first bomb at Central was not of German origin, but a homemade one in the Gents' toilet in November 1939. However, soon German bombs would be falling. Central suffered two major attacks. On 23rd November 1940 the town centre at Southampton was heavily bombed at the start of the *Southampton Blitz*.

Central was said to be ringed with fire as incendiary devices fell around. Some of these set fire to the Sports Club, and although staff including Stationmaster Collins, Inspector Yates, and Porter Mansbridge sought to fight the flames they were beaten back, partly by exploding ammunition from the rifle range. They were forced to take shelter under a table in the Ladies Waiting Room in the station while the bombs fell. Later on 30th November 1940 a bomb fell on the eastern end of the island platform causing extensive damage. Following these raids King George VI and Winston Churchill travelled to the town by train to see the damage for the themselves.

Worse was to come in a raid on 22nd July 1941, when two parachute bombs fell directly on the new down booking office completely demolishing it, and killing one person. Many parts of rest of the station were also heavily damaged.

Of course through all of this staff fought to maintain train services and deal with extra traffic. Not surprisingly many people sought safety outside the town. There were evacuations of women and children, but many also moved outside the town and commuted back in. To help with this train and bus tickets were made interchangeable between Central and Totton or Romsey. In one week in August 1941 400 tickets were exchanged at Central to cover journeys to Totton.

The embarkation of troops to France and the evacuation of troops from Dunkirk, when 23,000 troops arrived at or departed from the station meant a heavy workload for the staff. In 1942 Stationmaster Collins was awarded the British Empire Medal in recognition of the role he had played. Yet more was to come, because, before he retired in September 1944, he had also overseen the station's part in the D-Day landings.

Other events happened at the station during the war, some happy, some not. Women were of course now employed in new roles to take the place of men who had been called up, and in 1942 the staff celebrated the marriage of Miss. I.M. Frampton who had been portering at the station for eighteen months, as well as helping with the loudspeaker announcements. More sad was the death of a guard, Mr. G. Sandy, just as he was about to take charge of a train at the station on 17th November 1942.

Post-War

Like much of town, life gradually returned to normal after the war. Many parts of the town had been damaged, but people came back, and things began to move forwards. By 1947 services on the Bournemouth line had resumed their pre-war levels but some of the through expresses

Above: *Hampshire* DEMUs were introduced in 1957. In this undated view of No.1116, built in 1957 and strengthened to three-cars in 1959, is seen departing from Central for Millbrook with no yellow warning panels on the end, and carrying a tail lamp.
(Photographer Unknown)

Above and Below: The damage caused by the parachute bombs which fell on the station on the night of 22nd July 1941. In the photo above a crane is working to clear the debris and make safe the canopy of the island platform, which remains shorter than those on the other platforms to this day. In the background, ironically, the *Empire Theatre's* rooftop sign seems to have survived unscathed. Below, the gaping gap is seen where the only recently built down side booking office used to stand. This would not be rebuilt for nearly forty years. The damage to the power station building behind is also worth noting.

(Photos: R.K.Blencowe collection)

had yet to be restored. In 1948 the station became part of British Railways following Nationalisation.

Some of the war damage was repaired, but some was not. The down booking office was not finally replaced until 1980, while the Sports and Social Club was not at all. In addition a section of the canopy at the east end of the island platform also appears to have been removed, probably due to damage sustained during the war.

A *Santa Special* arrived at the station in 1952 with 500 children and parents on board, which was run in conjunction with the local *Mayes & Sons* store. 1953 saw the closure of the wartime control room with operations being moved to the Divisional Office that had been extended. Snow caused major disruption to services on 26th January 1954 when over 15 inches fell in 24 hours.

By mid-1954 there were around 150 timetabled train or light engine movements through the station daily. Classes of locomotives that could be observed included Bulleid Pacifics, *Nelsons, Arthurs*, N & U class Moguls, S15s, T9s, Q and Q1 classes, as well as H15 and M7 tank locomotives. In addition there were some of the new Standard 3 tanks and class 4 2-6-0 tender locomotives, as well as GWR engines.

Hampshire DEMUs took over many local services from 1957, and the same year there were also special trains run in conjunction with an international Girl Guides Rally. In 1958 it is recorded that 1,336,300 tickets were collected at the station and 732,776 issued, with 5,689 season tickets.

From Central to Southampton and Back

The 1960s were to see major changes once more at Central. In 1963 the Divisional Manager's Office was transferred to Wimbledon, while the following year the connection to the power station, which had been effectively disused since 1945, was removed. In the same year a major programme of repairs to the tunnel was started, which were to last for five months into 1965.

Electrification of the Bournemouth line was announced in 1964, and in 1965 it was confirmed that Central was to have a new set of up side station buildings. Clearly a boost to passenger numbers was required as ticket sales had fallen to 586,200 by 1965, under half of what it had been seven years earlier.

There was the sad sight of the demolition gangs moving in on the old up buildings in August 1966. Today it would be difficult to destroy such an architecturally interesting building to be replaced by, what was effectively an office block, but those were different times.

July 1967 saw the introduction of a full electric service on the Bournemouth line, and the end of steam. As a result, the previous months saw many railway enthusiasts heading for Southampton. There were also a number of specials run. The final day of steam was on 9th July, and the following day Central was renamed as simply Southampton.

The new station building was in use by 1968, and in 1971 the Divisional Office was demolished. Few alterations took place during the 1970s, but on 3rd April 1980 the new down booking office came into use. Then on 8th November 1981 the signal box closed, control having passed to Eastleigh. All the lines were now signalled for reversible running, with the fast and slow lines between Southampton and Millbrook being swopped.

Between 1983 and 1985 the tunnel was relined. Single line working was introduced while the work was carried out, and a narrow gauge railway line laid to allow the transport of materials to the work site.

A new booking hall building with a buffet and bookstall on the up side was opened in 1988. 1990 witnessed the first High Speed Train (HST) units in service on the cross country services to the north and Scotland.

Privatisation meant that the station was served by trains from four franchises. The London to Weymouth services are in the hands of *South West Trains*, which are also responsible for the services between Southampton and Portsmouth, and to Salisbury. *First Great Western* is responsible for through services from Portsmouth to Bristol and Cardiff. *Southern* runs trains to Brighton and

Left: The Divisional Office at Southampton Central seen here on 12th February 1971 shortly before it was demolished.
(Photo: R. Newman)

Right: A sad sight as the demolition gang works on dismantling the old clock-tower with most of the former up building already having been razed to the ground. One cannot imagine this being allowed today to such an iconic structure.

(Photo: H.W.Robinson
Copyright J.F.Hyde Steam Archive)

Below: *Merchant Navy* No. 35012 *United States Lines* arrives on platform one with a London train on 24th February 1967. It is certainly worth noting the period uniform of the platform staff.

(Photo: P.F.Bloxam)

Left: BR Standard class 4 mixed traffic 2-6-0 locomotive No.76063 enters Southampton tunnel on 19th March 1965 with a train of sleepers from the works at Redbridge. A major programme of repairs had been going on in the tunnel for the previous months, hence the gangers' trolley and permanent way materials on the left. Behind the tender is the former wartime control room.
(Photo: P.Pescod Copyright transporttreasury.co.uk)

London Victoria via Gatwick Airport. Finally *Cross Country* operates regular services to Manchester, the North East and Scotland.

Coming into the 21st century *Voyager* units were introduced on *Cross Country* services from 2001, and in 2003 the last HST ran on those services. On 29th May 2004 Southampton once more became Southampton Central, when it was renamed to overcome supposed confusion with Southampton Parkway. By then it was handling 300 passenger trains a day and 58 freight movements.

Passenger numbers have grown substantially, and the most recent figures have an estimated annual 5.6 million journeys either starting or finishing at Central. In 2009 a major programme of upgrades was announced for the station to provide improved facilities. Meanwhile between 2009 and 2010 work was done to lower the tunnel floor to allow new taller container trains to pass through it.

Right: Down side buildings in 1974. The gap where the booking office used to be is obvious. Meanwhile the range of cars in the car park is interesting as well as the *Red Funnel* bus to transfer passengers to the Isle of Wight ferries.

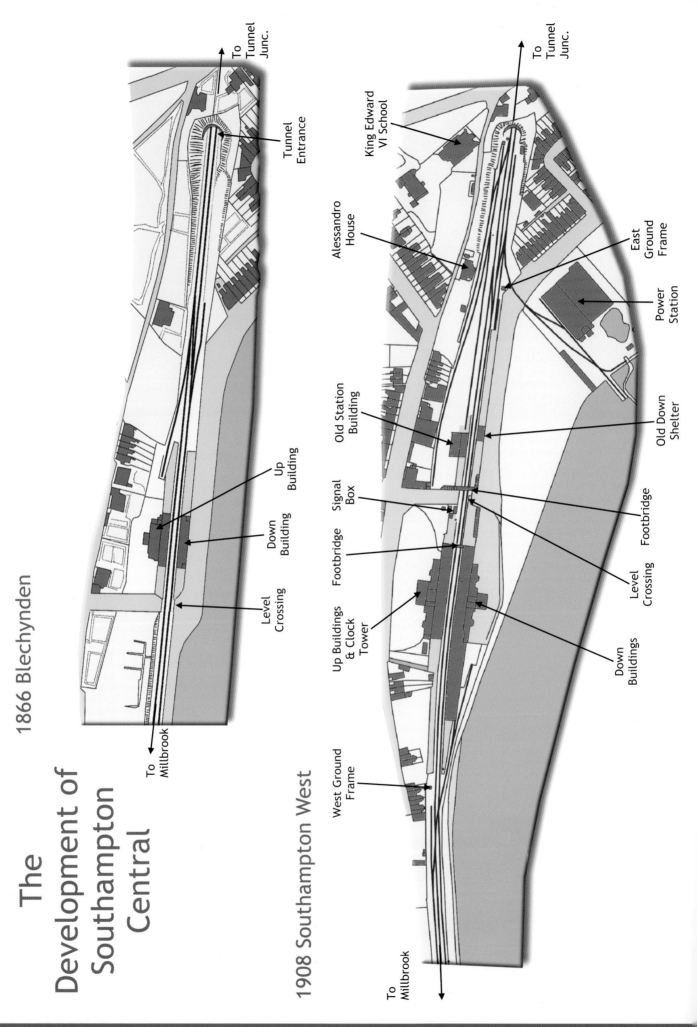

The Development of Southampton Central

1866 Blechynden

To Tunnel Junc.

Tunnel Entrance

Up Building

Down Building

Level Crossing

To Millbrook

1908 Southampton West

To Tunnel Junc.

King Edward VI School

Alessandro House

East Ground Frame

Power Station

Old Station Building

Old Down Shelter

Signal Box

Footbridge

Footbridge

Level Crossing

Up Buildings & Clock Tower

Down Buildings

West Ground Frame

To Millbrook

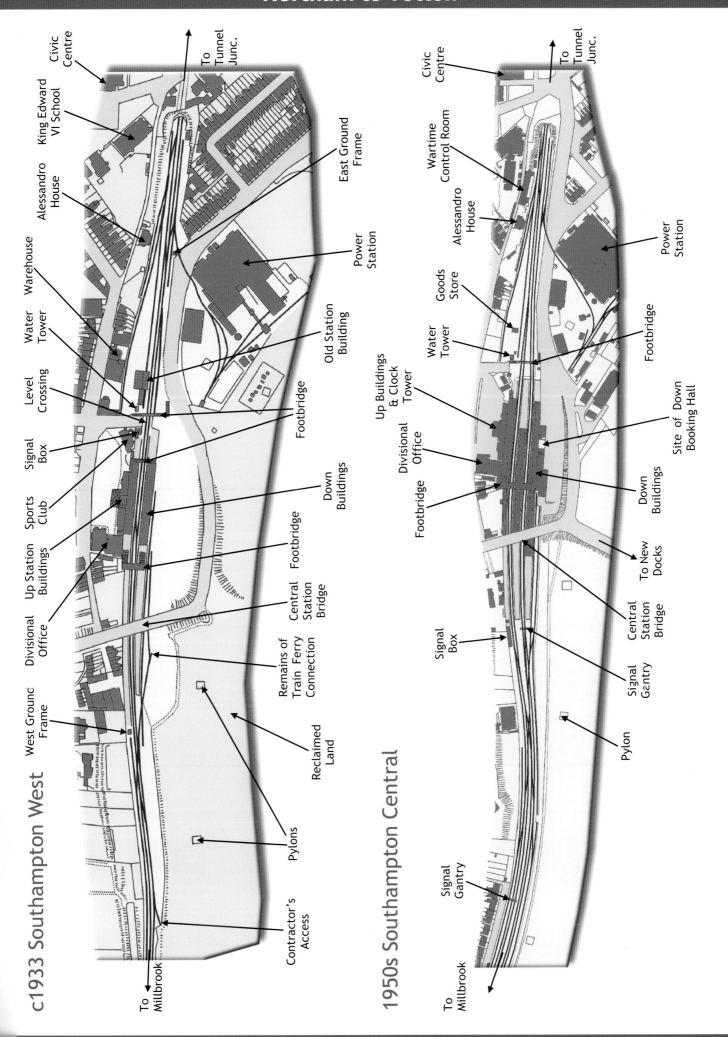

c1933 Southampton West

Civic Centre

King Edward VI School

Alessandro House

Warehouse

Water Tower

Level Crossing

Signal Box

Sports Club

Up Station Buildings

Divisional Office

West Ground Frame

To Millbrook

Contractor's Access

Pylons

Reclaimed Land

Remains of Train Ferry Connection

Central Station Bridge

Footbridge

Down Buildings

Footbridge

Old Station Building

Power Station

East Ground Frame

To Tunnel Junc.

1950s Southampton Central

Civic Centre

Wartime Control Room

Alessandro House

Goods Store

Water Tower

Up Buildings & Clock Tower

Divisional Office

Footbridge

Signal Box

To Millbrook

Signal Gantry

Pylon

Signal Gantry

Central Station Bridge

To New Docks

Down Buildings

Site of Down Booking Hall

Footbridge

Power Station

To Tunnel Junc.

Right: The sad sight of *Alessandro House* on 9th April 1973, for many years the residence of the stationmaster, having been purchased in 1887 at a total price of £606 including repairs. It was subsequentley used for other purposes, before being demolished in November 1975.

(Photo: K.G.Carr Collection Copyright P.Fidczuk)

Left: I'll admit that the main reason for including this photograph of Standard class 4 No. 76014 departing Central is sentimental, as anyone who attended King Edward VI School in Southampton of my generation, or older, will recognise the photographer as a member of staff who was something of an institution. 'Uncle Bullar' gave me this photo to publish as part of my original articles on Southampton's stations, and I'm pleased at last to be able to do so.

However, it does serve an historical purpose, because being a pre-1964 view the spur that led across the road to the power station, although out of use for many years, can still be seen just to the right of the down signals. Standing or sitting above the tunnel entrance was an excellent place to observe the movements of trains through the station. The signal being pulled 'off' gave warning of an approaching train, while there was also a satisfying 'clunk' as it returned to danger.

(Photo: R.G.Avent)

Right: Rebuilt *West Country* No.34004 *Yeovil* approaches the tunnel mouth with a train on 24th February 1967. By this time the connection to the power station had been removed. A colour light signal had now replaced the semaphore arm on the down gantry and the conductor rails have been laid.
(Photo: P.F.Bloxam)

Above: Ex-GWR *Hall* class No.6923 *Croxteth Hall* enters Southampton on 26th March 1964. Note the near-empty goods yard occupied by Engineer's department wagons.

(Photo: P.F.Bloxam)

Above: *Merchant Navy* No.35012 *United States Lines* stands at the end of platform one at Central on 24th February 1967.

(Photo: P.F.Bloxam)

Above: Another *Merchant Navy*, No.35026 *Lamport & Holt Line*, takes water at the down end of platform three on 10th June 1965.
(Photo: P.F.Bloxam)

Above: The classic view of locomotives departing from Central heading down to Millbrook under the signal gantry. Only this time it is ex-LBSCR H2 *Atlantic* class 4-4-2 No.32421 *South Foreland* departing in the snow in January 1954. The gantry was preserved as part of the National Collection.
(Photo: S.C.Townroe Copyright Colour-Rail BRS990)

Above: *West Country* No.34037 *Clovelly* arrives at Central with a Waterloo train on 30th March 1967.   (Photo: P.F.Bloxam)

Above: An unidentified *Lord Nelson* approaches Southampton Central past the signal box on 18th June 1955 with a train from Bournemouth West for Waterloo.   (Photo: Leslie Freeman Copyright transporttreasury.co.uk)

Left: The first mainline diesel in the country, No.10000 built by the LMS in 1947. It and No.10001 were transferred to Southern Region in 1953 for comparison trials, and it is seen here approaching Central with a train from Bournemouth.
(Photographer Unknown)

Right: A later generation of diesel locomotives at Southampton Central on 13th April 1988 as two class 47s are photographed at the Millbrook end of the station. No.47555 departs with a P&O special on connection with the naming of class 37 No.37358 *P&O Containers*, while No.47270 passes with a tanker train from Fawley.
(Photo: R.Silsbury)

Left: *Berkshire* DEMU, by now class 205 No.205028 departs from Southampton Central on the 4.24pm Southampton to Portsmouth Harbour, passing 4-TC unit No.8016 on the down line on 5th July 1988.
(Photo: R.Silsbury)

Above: A new down booking office was finally completed in 1980, only 39 years after the original was blown-up. It is seen here in January 2011.

Right: Only the stub of a siding remains on the down side after work to lower trackbed in the tunnel to increase the loading gauge, as *Desiro* unit No.444026 crosses onto the up line through the tunnel on 20th January 2011.

Left: *Overline House* completed in 1968; a characterless replacement for the 1895 building.

Right: Having built a large office block it was soon realised that increased passenger facilities were needed, after all it is a station, so in 1988 an enlarged booking hall was opened. It is seen here on 20th January 2011.

Train-spotting between Central and Millbrook

Above: In January 1954 *Battle of Britain* class No.34089 *602 Squadron* ploughs through the snow as it approaches Southampton Central from Millbrook.   (Photo: S.C.Townroe Copyright Colour-Rail BRS985)

Above: In more clement weather *Lord Nelson* No.30851 *Sir Francis Drake* departs from Central on 27th December 1960 with three Southampton icons in the background, namely the Civic Centre clock, the old Central clock tower and the signal gantry. Any similarity between the London Midland and Scottish Railway's (LMS) *Royal Scots* and the *Lord Nelsons* is not co-incidental as the LMS borrowed the *Nelson's* designer, R.E.L.Maunsell's, drawings to base their design on. Sadly only one *Nelson* is preserved.
                                             (Photo: P.F.Bloxam)

Above: A few months previously U class Mogul No.31629 departs with a through train for the old MSWJR on 27th August 1960.
(Photo: P.F.Bloxam)

Above: Towards the end of steam on Southern Region *West Country* No.34013 *Okehampton* storms away from Central on 2nd January 1967, note the second coach in the 'new' British Rail blue and grey livery.
(Photo: P.F.Bloxam)

Above: Moving down towards Millbrook U class Mogul No.31795 on an up freight approaches Southampton Central on 7th November 1959. This locomotive was originally the K class 2-6-4 tank locomotive No.A795 *River Medway*, built in 1925. It was rebuilt into the form seen here, along with other members of the class, in 1928 following the crash of A800 *River Cray* at Sevenoaks in 1927. In the background is the Cracknore Road footbridge. (Photo: P.F.Bloxam)

Above: On the other side of the footbridge, British Railways Standard class 4 2-6-0 No.76010 passes the houses on Saxon Road with an up freight at 1.15pm on 5th January 1965. This locomotive pulled the last steam-hauled train on the Swanage branch under British Rail on 4th September 1966. It was near here that an exploding bomb rendered the line impassable on the night of 30th November 1940.
(Photo: P.F.Bloxam)

Above: Now nearer to Millbrook, ex-GWR 43xx 2-6-0 No.6391 passes with a train probably bound for Basingstoke and Reading on 7th November 1959.   (Photo: P.F.Bloxam)

Above: An unidentified *West Country* has just passed through Millbrook station on 27th December 1960 as it approaches Central. Note the interesting observatory on the top of the house in the background, that must have had quite a view.

(Photo: P.F.Bloxam)

Millbrook

Above: BR Standard 5 mixed traffic 4-6-0 No. 73112 *Morgan le Fay* stands at Millbrook light engine having just emerged from the New Docks on 27th December 1960. (Photo: P.F.Bloxam)

Departing from Blechynden, or Southampton West, station before the 1930s a train would have run along the shoreline first heading west, and then curving north west. On the south side of the tracks was the seawall with a promenade, while to the north were the gardens of villas that overlooked the water at this point. Just after the tracks curved north west they were crossed by a footbridge at the end of, what is now, Cracknore Road giving access to the promenade.

All this changed in the 1930s with the reclamation of the land for the New Docks. Now Southampton Central lies half a mile inland, and Millbrook station over a quarter of a mile from the water's edge. It was also at this time that the track was quadrupled for the three-quarters of a mile between the two stations.

Origins of Millbrook Station

A notice appeared in the *Hampshire Advertiser* of the 29th December 1855 advertising a school for young ladies at *Sutherland House*. What makes this of interest is that the premises are said to be near the 'Millbrook Railway Station', except that this did not officially exist until November 1861!

It is possible that, as in the case of Totton which will be examined later, a semi-official stopping point did exist near Millbrook, maybe in connection with the nearby foundry which closed in 1854, but without any substantial facilities. Of course it could

also be that the reference was to Blechynden or Redbridge. However, the proposed A&RR and Shirley Railways, as well as a petition from residents, seems to have galvanised the LSWR board into action. On 1st November 1861, a station was opened opposite the site of the old Foundry. This was said to be a wooden structure 'similar to Portswood'.

At first the facilities were indeed basic, but soon these improved. Gas lighting was put in place, supplied from the nearby works of the *Shirley Gas Co*. However, the station does not appear to have been a complete success because in 1866 it was decided it should be closed and replaced with a station at Nursling, but happily this did not occur.

Later, in 1869, a short siding was added at the back of the up platform which had a trailing connection to the up line on land given by *Vincent & Elliot*. There was also a signal box at the level crossing at the west end of the station. The crossing led to the old foundry wharf, where ships

London and South Western Ry.
787
TO
MILLBROOK

Above: On 23rd February 1924 an unidentified T6 class 4-4-0, still in LSWR livery, heads towards Millbrook with a train for Romsey possibly containing ex-MSWJR stock. The proximity of the line to the water's edge at this time can be clearly seen as well as the promenade built by the S&DR. (Photo: Copyright HMRS D.S.Foukes-Roberts collection)

built in the foundry were dragged across the road to be launched. This had now become a popular bathing spot, along with the promenade.

Under the LSWR

During the 1870s *W. Cookson and Co.* were operating their coal merchant's business from the station. Improvements were also made to the station, including the provision of toilets in 1875. In the 1880s a goods shed was built along with a loading dock. A footbridge was constructed in 1896, and the signal box rebuilt west of the crossing, while another siding was added the following year.

By 1909 fifteen down passenger trains called at the station each weekday most to Bournemouth or Weymouth, but also to destinations such as Lymington, Andover, and Totton. In the other direction trains travelled mainly to Southampton Town or Portsmouth, but also to Eastleigh, and two evening services through to Waterloo. Meanwhile the area around the station had been changing. Originally built on the edge of the development along the River Test, now more of the area had been built up.

During the early years of the 20th century the goods yard to the west of the station was developed, with land being purchased and drained. Two long trailing sidings were laid on the up side west of the station giving access to three short sidings which formed the goods yard behind the up

Above: Possibly the earliest known view of Millbrook station showing the level crossing nearest the camera, along with the original signal box, booking office, and waiting shelters, all of wooden construction. Wagons can be seen in the siding and also note the malt kiln. The original wooden platform had been extended in 1887. (Photo: Copyright National Railway Museum/SSPL)

Above: This later view probably dates from the 1900s as by now the goods yard is being developed. *Holden and Son's* coal office is in the centre of the picture. To the left is the entrance to the wooden station booking office, while on the extreme right is the premises of *Toogoods* seeds which is still a landmark today. (Photographer Unknown)

platform, as well as the small goods shed. The signal box frame was extended in September 1908 to control the new yard.

The Southern

Under the Southern the goods yard continued to be enlarged with four additional sidings laid in 1926 to accommodate 120 trucks. In addition, a new entrance to the yard was provided, as well as a cattle pen and loading dock. The following year a large new goods warehouse was provided with two additional sidings and also a goods office. By this time too, *Toogoods* seed merchants had built their premises across the road from the yard. The building dominated the skyline, particularly from 1935 when they added a neon sign.

Toogoods were responsible for around 6,000 consignments of goods a month from the station. Nearby the *Eucryl* factory, which manufactured *Dentrifice* paste and powder, handled 2,000 consignments a year in the 1930s.

Major change came at Millbrook with the quadrupling of the line from Southampton West in 1935. The down platform was rebuilt and lengthened as an island platform serving the up and down through lines, and the up platform and buildings were demolished. New station buildings and canopies were built on the single platform, which also had a flower border with rose trees.

Above: Millbrook station buildings seen from the up side in the early 1960s show the station after the re-building of 1935. The single island platform served the up and down fast lines. (Photo: Lens of Sutton Association)

Left: A view of the approach to the rebuilt Millbrook station from the Central end in the 1960s.
(Photo: Lens of Sutton Association)

Meanwhile the footbridge was replaced with an extended ramped bridge to maintain the right of way across the tracks. On 2nd June 1935 the old signal box was replaced with a new box with a 70-lever Westinghouse frame, and level crossing was also closed.

During the Second World War Millbrook suffered little air raid damage, although incendiary devices fell on the station on the night of 30th November 1940, but it served as a major coal dump for emergency supplies for the town. However, the station was damaged during the victory celebrations when revelers used wood from the fencing and footbridge to build a bonfire. In 1941 there were still fourteen down passenger trains calling going to Bournemouth, Weymouth, Fawley, Romsey and Andover, but by 1947 this number had actually gone down to thirteen.

Nationalisation

Nationalisation made little difference to Millbrook, and life at the station carried on. However, in the 1960s things began to change. The station was made unstaffed from 22nd May 1966, and on 15th July 1967 the goods yard was closed. By this time the lines through the station had been electrified. Under the new service Millbrook was served by an hourly service in each direction supplemented during peak periods.

Another major change at this point was the conversion of the former goods yard into a *Freightliner* container terminal that opened on 29th January 1968. That same year the old buildings and canopies were demolished due to vandalism, and replaced with very basic shelters.

On 8th November 1981 the signal box was closed, and the station simply became an unstaffed platform. Today the station is served by the hourly *South West Trains* Salisbury-Southampton circular in each direction.

However, it now occupies a very isolated site bounded on one side by the Western Approach Road, which at this point is a dual carriageway with a total of six lanes, plus a two lane slip road. All of these have to be crossed on an extended station footbridge. Even so still around 29,000 passenger journeys start or finish from the station each year.

To the south are the freight lines which give access to the New Docks just to the west of the station. Beyond this, within the confines of the docks themselves, is a vast car park for imported vehicles. However, still the site gives an air of desolation, and a complete contrast to the small station on the water's edge it started off as.

Right: The new signal box at Millbrook.
(Photo: Lens of Sutton Association)

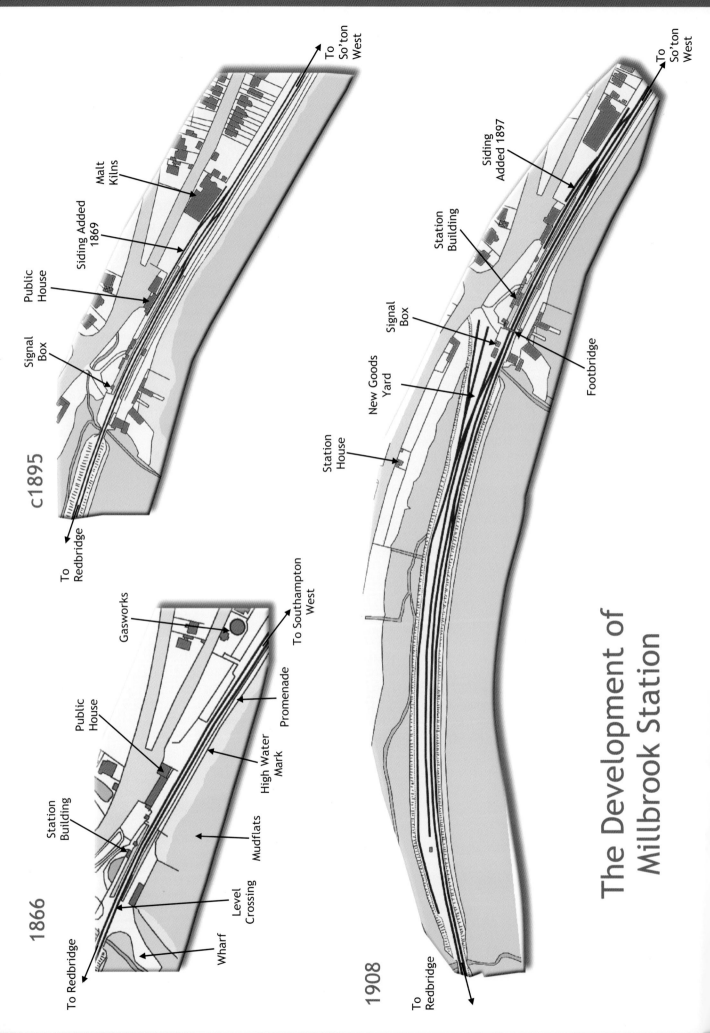

c1895

To So'ton West

Malt Kilns

Siding Added 1869

Public House

Signal Box

To Redbridge

1866

Gasworks

Public House

Station Building

To Redbridge

Wharf

Level Crossing

Mudflats

High Water Mark

Promenade

To Southampton West

To So'ton West

Siding Added 1897

Station Building

Signal Box

Footbridge

New Goods Yard

Station House

1908

To Redbridge

The Development of Millbrook Station

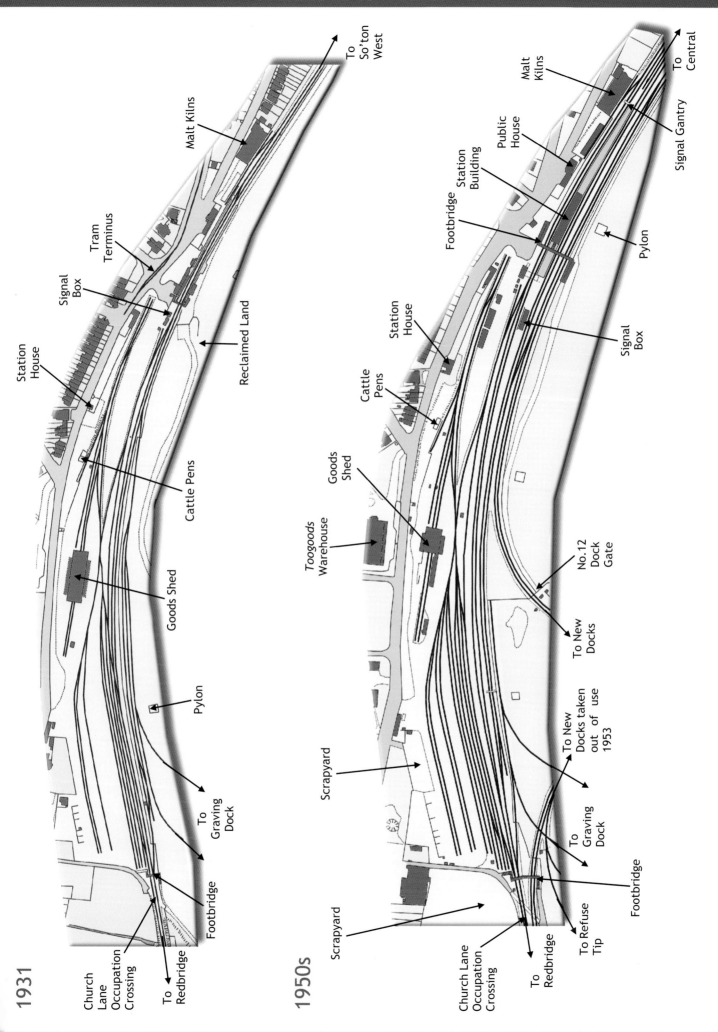

1931

Malt Kilns

Tram Terminus

Signal Box

Station House

To So'ton West

Reclaimed Land

Cattle Pens

Goods Shed

Pylon

To Graving Dock

Footbridge

Church Lane Occupation Crossing

To Redbridge

1950s

Malt Kilns

Public House

Station Building

Footbridge

Station House

Cattle Pens

Goods Shed

Toogoods Warehouse

Scrapyard

Scrapyard

Church Lane Occupation Crossing

To Redbridge

Signal Gantry

To Central

Pylon

Signal Box

No.12 Dock Gate

To New Docks

To New Docks taken out of use 1953

To Graving Dock

Footbridge

To Refuse Tip

Left: On 7th November 1959 *West Country* Pacific No. 34098 *Templecombe*, built by BR at Brighton in 1949, and seen in its rebuilt state in the frontispiece, passes Millbrook with a Brighton to Cardiff train. Behind the locomotive can be seen the vans of *MacFarlane Lang's Biscuits and Cakes*, later *McVitie's*. Compare this scene to the top photo opposite.
(Photo: P.F.Bloxam)

Below: *West Country* No. 34036 *Westward Ho!* built in 1946, rebuilt in 1960, passes the signal box and under the footbridge with a Waterloo train on the afternoon of 24th February 1967.
(Photo: P.F.Bloxam)

Below: An unidentified Mogul heads towards Millbrook past the goods yard on 7th November 1959. Note the *Esso* tank wagons and open wagons loaded with timber and covered with tarpaulins. The goods shed can also be clearly seen.
(Photo: P.F.Bloxam)

Top: The new Western Approach Road has swept much away in this view of class 33 No.33108 passing Millbrook with a Portsmouth to Cardiff train on 5th August 1984.

(Photographer Unknown)

Right: Trees have grown in the 27 years between this view, taken in January 2011, and the photo above.

Below: In 1968 a *Freightliner* depot was established on the old goods yard site and can be seen in this view in January 2011. Meanwhile class 66 No.66146 emerges from the container berths with a train on the left. The former *Toogoods* building can still be seen on the right.

Redbridge

Above: Redbridge works shunter *USA* class DS233, formerly No.30061, is seen at Redbridge on 9th March 1966 with the signal box in the background. Despite surviving so near to the end of steam, sadly it was scrapped in 1967.

(Photo: Copyright Colour-Rail 342266)

Travelling on from Millbrook the line first crossed Millbrook Creek, before curving along the shoreline until heading south west. Church Creek was then bridged, and next came an occupation crossing at Church Lane leading to Millbrook Point. This had a footbridge added in 1920, and one is still *in-situ* today. To the north of the line the landscape was rather more rural until the 20th century.

Today to the north lies the sprawling Millbrook estate, while to the south, land was re-claimed for the New Docks and the George V Graving Dock. Along here during World War Two new connections were laid on the down side, to allow trains to access the New Docks from Bournemouth and Salisbury.

The tracks now traversed Millbrook Marsh, where originally to the seaward side the line was used as a rifle range, before an Isolation hospital was built on Millbrook Point in the early 1900s. Later a sewage works was constructed on the site. Now curving north west again the line crossed Tanner's Brook, and beyond this Millbrook village itself was passed on the north side, again all now vanished under roads, industrial estates, and housing.

South of the line there was farmland and the remains of the old canal, all swept away with the building of the container port in the 1970s. In 1972 the Maritime

Freightliner Terminal opened on the south side of the line, with the connections to Redbridge making use of the alignment of the former wartime docks lines. A new access road to the container berths also crosses the line at this point.

Approaching the village of Redbridge to the south of the line there was Redbridge Wharf. Here there was a *Vitriol* factory, *Vitriol* being another name for sulphuric acid, which is used in iron and steel-making, as well as in the manufacture of fertilizers and detergents. Later a gunpowder factory was based here, before it was taken over by the Redbridge Permanent Way works, which will be looked at later. Again all this has disappeared under the new container berths. Now the train enters Redbridge station a mile and three-quarters from Millbrook.

Redbridge Station

It was always intended that Redbridge was to be the first station out from Southampton on the S&DR, as it also marked the end of the double track section through from Southampton Junction. Redbridge itself was the first bridging point over the River Test, and was even mentioned in the Doomsday Book. Later it had its own monastery, but was also known for shipbuilding. At the end of the 18th century a new river bridge was

Right: *King Arthur* class No.30788 *Sir Urre of the Mount* passes over the Church Lane occupation crossing, with a train for Waterloo, early in 1962. Built in 1925 it was destined to be withdrawn that February. On the left is the remains of one of the wartime connections into the docks.

(Photo: Copyright Colour-Rail 341605)

constructed here, which can still be seen. This was also the end of the Andover Canal, later converted to the A&RR.

When opened, with the rest of the S&DR on 1st June 1847, Redbridge seems to have had two platforms and a brick-built station building on the up side to the standard S&DR design. At the western end of the station there was a level crossing giving access to Redbridge Wharf.

The double track possibly extended beyond Redbridge across the viaduct over the River Test, as there is no mention of the viaduct being widened when the line to Beaulieu Road was doubled in August 1857. By 1859 there were significant moves towards the building of the line from Andover to Redbridge, as already mentioned on page 11. Therefore, it seems surprising that around this time the LSWR proposed to close the station. This was

said by the Company to be due to the proposed new station at Totton just over a half a mile distant. However, local speculation was that it was more to do with not permitting the A&RR to use the LSWR's station.

Having relented the LSWR built new facilities on the up platform in 1862 after installing gas lighting in 1860. Finally on 6th March 1865 the new line to Romsey was opened and Redbridge became a junction. At this point there seem to have been two signal boxes at Redbridge, the first west of the occupation crossing controlling the junction, while a second at Test Gates controlled the crossing over the causeway on the line to Romsey. By 1880 there were two sidings on the up side, and a loading dock, the latter having been established in connection with an agricultural show in 1869. Meanwhile, on the down side there was a siding with a headshunt, as well as a connection into the *Vitriol* factory.

Left: A view of Redbridge station looking east in May 1950. The footbridge had been replaced in 1937 with one that also allows access to the works as well as the down platform. Note the tall junction signals to help with visibility.
(Photo: K.G.Carr collection Copyright P.Fidczuk)

Left: The precise date of the building of this signal box at Redbridge is something of a mystery. As Redbridge was at the end of the double track from Southampton when the line opened. There must presumably have been a signal box or block post somewhere in the area. Certainly there is a signal box marked at the new junction with the A&RR on the 1866 map, however, it is unlikely to be this one, at least not in this form.

But this box did have features in common with the box at Southampton West which was built, or rebuilt, in 1895. Most likely, in the author's opinion, is that this box dates from the doubling of the line to Romsey in 1884, and was closed in 1982.

(Photo: D.J.Powell collection Copyright Kidderminster Railway Museum)

Station and Works

In the 1880s the LSWR acquired Redbridge Wharf from William Shawland, and established a works there for the production of sleepers and other components for the permanent way. Part of the site was also occupied by a Linseed Oil factory, as well as the *Vitriol* plant already mentioned. By now the original wooden viaduct over the Test was in need of replacement. So in 1883 a new cast iron bridge was constructed slightly south of the original. However, it was nearly short-lived as a storm in September 1883 almost washed the line away.

Passenger accommodation was improved at a cost of £1,071, with an additional building on the up platform in 1882. March 1884 saw the doubling of the line between Redbridge and Romsey, and the platforms lengthened.

Other features also enhanced the passenger experience as a writer for the *Hampshire Advertiser* made clear in his appreciation of the flower beds at Redbridge in 1890. Further improvement came with the addition of a footbridge in 1895. Later, in 1898, the *Schultz Gunpowder Co.* was established on the site of the old *Vitriol* works with its own connection to the down line.

An interesting development might have been the conversion of the junction at Redbridge into a triangle. Several of the proposals for the Andover to Redbridge line had suggested it, as well as later proposals for the line to Stone Point. However, in 1906 the LSWR themselves took out powers to do the necessary work, but it was never completed, the powers lapsing in 1917.

By 1909 there was a significant number of trains calling at

Left: Looking towards Millbrook on 4th April 1960 the down shelter can clearly be seen, and in the distance on the right is the Foundry. Approaching light engine is H15 class 4-6-0 No.30522 built in 1924. Meanwhile passing through the up platform is an unidentified Pacific with a train for Waterloo.

(Photo: R.Amos Copyright Kidderminster Railway Museum)

Left: L1 class 4-4-0 No. 31789 approaches Redbridge on 23rd May 1953 with a train for Waterloo composed of ex-LSWR stock. Note the disused cattle dock on the right.
(Photo: R.C.Riley Copyright transporttreasury.co.uk)

Redbridge. In the down direction alone there were 38 booked passenger trains due to stop there. These were heading to Bournemouth, Weymouth, Romsey, Salisbury, Andover, Bristol, Cardiff, Totton and Lymington, including two trains worked by the MSWJR. There were also ten down goods trains. In 1922 the gunpowder factory closed and plans were made for an extension to Redbridge works, but this was to be completed by the SR.

The Southern

Initially the days of life under the Southern seem to be ones of contraction. Sunday services to the station were suspended with the start of the winter timetable in

September 1926, and in 1927 Redbridge came under the jurisdiction of the stationmaster at Millbrook.

In 1930 the two sidings parallel to the Romsey line began to serve the timber yard of *Bryce, White and Co.*. Meanwhile the level crossing on this length of line was closed on 18th November 1930 when the new road flyover came into use.

It is always good to get a glimpse of the human story of what went on at these stations, and occasions such as retirements or departures often provide such an opportunity. In 1931 signalman W.Ridges retired after 48 years service to the railway, 33 of them at Redbridge,

Left: The approach to Redbridge station on 23rd April 1978 with the old S&DR building on the left, and the later 1880s building on the right.

(Photo: R.Newman)

Right: The extended building of 1882 has been demolished in the last few years, and now only the old S&DR building remains in this view takn in January 2011.

Redbridge Station in 1866

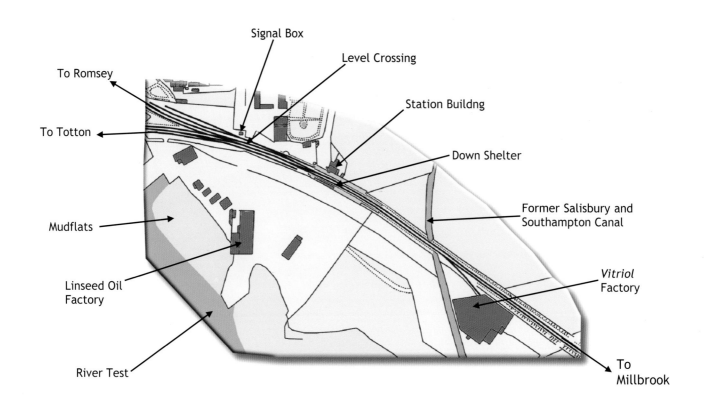

while in 1934 stationmaster Mr.H.C.Gray moved on to Wareham, and was presented with a pipe and tobacco pouch from the Redbridge staff. There were other less happy occasions too such as the death of signalman J.A. Birkett in November 1932 aged 56.

The Second World War

Being slightly removed from the centre of Southampton did not prevent Redbridge from being a target during the war, and on 19th June 1940 the works was damaged by a bomb blast destroying a large quantity of sleepers. Later the new connections to the docks, previously mentioned, came into use on 28th March 1943. A sand drag was added to their west end near the station in December the same year.

During the war, in 1941, the down passenger service consisted of only fourteen trains, with four trains booked to traverse the line to Romsey. However, one of these was now a through train to Exeter. Following the conflict in 1946-47 the junction and track were renewed with track circuits, and the alignment of the approaches to the viaduct were improved.

Nationalisation

After the war train services were gradually restored with sixteen down trains calling at the station in 1947. Still only four of these were to use the line to Romsey. In March 1953 the former docks lines were taken out of use as running lines, although at least one was left in-situ. The following year the cattle dock spur was also removed.

In 1964 the Test viaduct was replaced once more, this time in reinforced concrete on the alignment of the original 1847 bridge. By now passenger trains at Redbridge on the Romsey line were in the hands of *Hampshire* DEMUs, and an hourly service to Andover formed the backbone of the schedule. This combined with two trains still making the journey to Fawley, and the trains to Bournemouth, made a total of 30 down passenger trains calling at the station every weekday.

The up sidings were taken out of use in November 1966. By that time the electrification programme was proceeding. In July 1967 Redbridge was served by the hourly slow trains on the new electric service as well as by trains to Salisbury, Bristol and Cardiff. Nineteen down trains called each day on the Bournemouth line, and eighteen going to Romsey or beyond by 1980.

On 23rd February 1982 the signal box closed, and was later demolished. Meanwhile in 1989 the Civil Engineering works also closed. On the station the down shelter was replaced with a shelter. The up building lasted into the 21st century, before it too was demolished.

Today the station is tucked away in a small enclave hemmed in by the Western Approach Road and the container port. It is served by the hourly Salisbury-Southampton-Salisbury service in each direction, and has an estimated number of passenger journeys commencing or ending at the station of around 25,000 annually. In many ways, like Millbrook, a sad reflection on what once was.

Left: On 23rd April 1978 *Hampshire* DEMU No.1125 on the 8.35am from Portsmouth Harbour to Salisbury departs from the station.
(Photo: R.Newman)

Right: On the same day the 9.40am from Salisbury approaches Redbridge. Note the barriers on the level crossing. Behind the train there is the new flyover, the timber yard, and the railway cottages behind the signal box.
(Photo: R.Newman)

Left: In January 2011 an unidentified *Voyager* unit passes over the former level crossing as it enters Redbridge en-route to Central and the north.

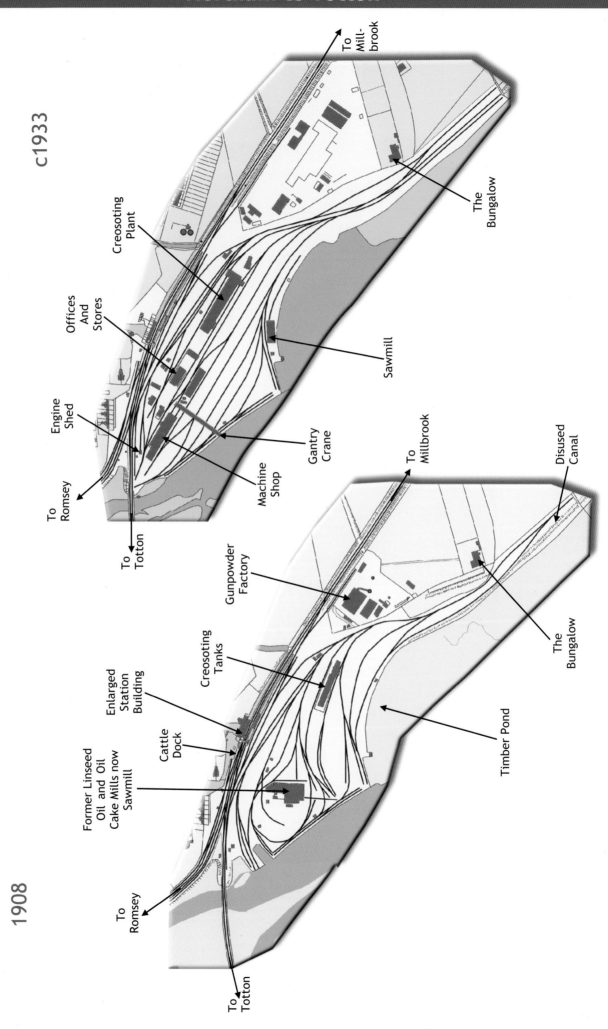

Development of Redbridge Wharf and Works

c1933

To Mill-brook

Creosoting Plant

The Bungalow

Offices And Stores

Sawmill

Engine Shed

Gantry Crane

To Romsey

Machine Shop

To Totton

To Millbrook

Disused Canal

Gunpowder Factory

The Bungalow

Enlarged Station Building

Creosoting Tanks

Cattle Dock

Former Linseed Oil and Oil Cake Mills now Sawmill

Timber Pond

To Romsey

To Totton

1908

1950s

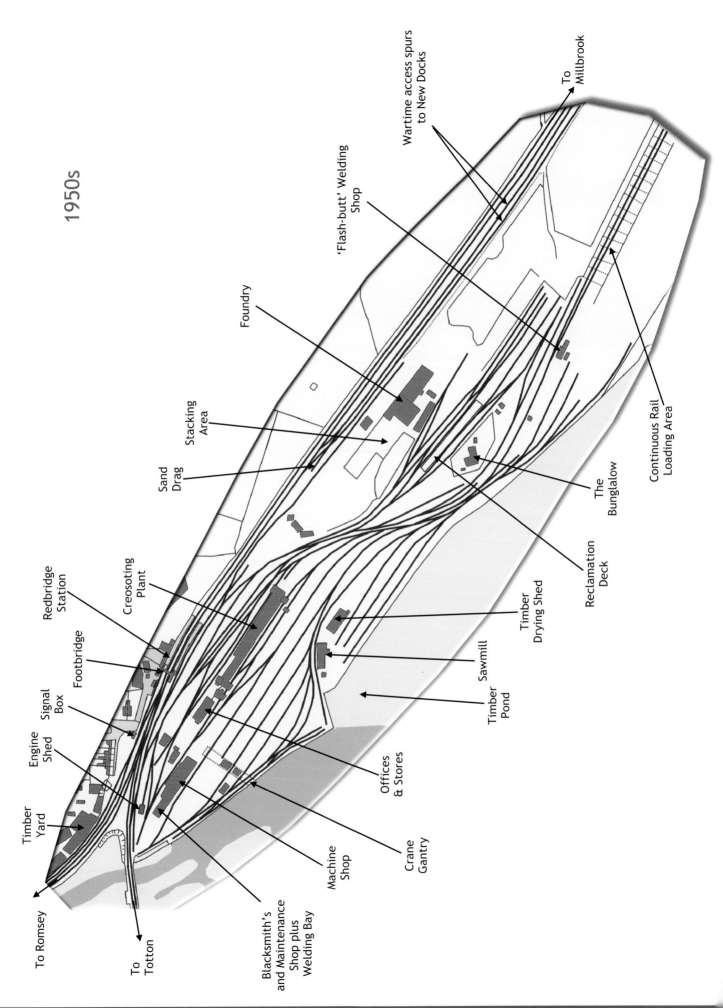

To Millbrook

Wartime access spurs to New Docks

'Flash-butt' Welding Shop

Foundry

Continuous Rail Loading Area

Stacking Area

Sand Drag

The Bungalow

Reclamation Deck

Redbridge Station

Creosoting Plant

Footbridge

Timber Drying Shed

Signal Box

Sawmill

Engine Shed

Timber Pond

Offices & Stores

Timber Yard

Crane Gantry

Machine Shop

To Romsey

To Totton

Blacksmith's and Maintenance Shop plus Welding Bay

Left: Ex-LSWR sleeper wagon based at Redbridge pictured c1926.
(Photo: Copyright HMRS Ray Chorley collection)

Redbridge Works

When the LSWR acquired Redbridge wharf in 1881 it was first used as a delivery point and storage site for permanent way materials. This was a cheaper option than having them delivered to Eling Wharf. Rails first started to be delivered towards the end of 1881, as part of the doubling of the line to Romsey, and by 1882 additional sidings were laid at the station.

Creosote tanks were installed in 1882 for the treatment of sleepers. These were roofed over in 1883. Further sidings were also laid and a steam crane acquired the same year, with extra land being purchased the following year. Later more land was acquired for eight cottages near the station in 1887.

In the centre of the wharf site was the *Dixon & Cardus Oil and Cake Mills*, which had been established in 1853 and lasted at the site until 1899 when the company moved to Northam. After this the building was adapted by the LSWR for use as a sawmill.

A timber pond was also established where wood could be seasoned before being sawn and treated. The logs were floated round from the wharf and chained together until being lifted and transferred to the sawmill.

Rail access to the works was provided in 1895 before then materials were shifted around the site by horses. Steam cranes were subsequently used for shunting, and later still locomotives such as class B4s were used. However, it seems that there was not a dedicated shunting locomotive for the works until the days of the Southern.

At the north east corner of the site was the *Vitriol* plant, which had been established in 1863 and lasted until 1892, and had its own private siding. Later the *Shultz Gunpowder Co.* was established in 1898 on the east side of the old *Vitriol* site. Its operations lasted until 1922; again this had a private siding off the down line on a trailing connection.

Grouping

The Southern made a significant investment in the works

at Redbridge shortly after Grouping, following decisions that had been made by the LSWR in 1922. Pressure creosoting was introduced in 1924, with a new building being constructed to house the equipment. At its height Redbridge handled nearly a million sleepers annually. A new gantry crane was also provided to load and unload wagons.

Between 1923 and 1924 a new stores building and machine shop were built, along with a sawmill, which replaced the one in the former oil factory that was demolished. In addition, a foundry was created, initially at the west end of the works, then moving to the site of the old gunpowder factory in 1933.

Class C14 0-4-0 tank locomotive No.745 was assigned to the works as a dedicated shunting locomotive in 1927, being numbered 77s. It took up residence in a loco shed that had been converted from a former pump house beside the down Bournemouth line, between the works and the junction.

In the midst of this railway works a private asphalt works was established by *Scientific Roads (Southern) Ltd*, which continued to operate until 1948. This was built on the site of the old *Vitriol* plant, and had its own siding for bitumen tank wagons.

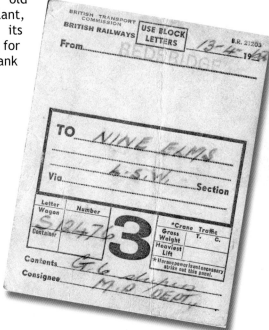

Left: Loading sleepers in Redbridge works.
(Photographer Unknown)

C14 No.77s had left by this time too, to go to Town Quay, and was replaced first by O2s allocated from Eastleigh, then, from October 1962, by *USA* class No.30061, renumbered DS233. This lasted until March 1967 when DS233 was withdrawn, and replaced by diesels. Initially Drewry 0-6-0 shunters were employed, but a class 07 from Southampton docks would sometimes appear. Later these were superceded by 08 or 09 class shunters until the closure of the works.

Further investment was made in the works with a new flash-welding plant installed in 1962-63. Concrete sleepers began to replace wooden ones, and so the use of the creosoting plant declined, although it was not demolished until 1978.

Nationalisation

Further expansion followed Nationalisation. Continuously welded rail had first been developed at the turn of the 20th century, but aside from on the London Underground little use had been made of them in the UK. However, following the Second World War, a 'flash-butt' welding plant was commissioned at Redbridge in 1950 along with a new foundry on the old gunpowder factory site.

One domestic enclave that survived in the middle of the works was *The Bungalow*, which had originally been built for the manager of the powder factory. This lasted until 1961 when it was demolished.

Changing technology also brought improved facilities, with a new machine shop being built in 1971 to handle the manganese-steel rails then being introduced. In 1977 a modern sand-plant was constructed at the foundry to increase production.

Redbridge works was finally closed on 3rd March 1989. At its height it occupied 42 acres of land, with around eight miles of sidings. In its latter years it provided employment for just over 160 workers, contributing significantly to the economy of the area. Now most of the site has become a car park for vehicles passing through the docks.

Above: At least they didn't have to transport the track components far when it came to relaying the permanent way in connection with the new viaduct over the River Test. The track gang can be seen hard at work in this scene from 31st May 1964. In the centre of the background the new viaduct can be seen, the old one lying to the left just to the right of the engine shed. Note the wagons on the left stacked high with sleepers, presumably shunted up from the storage piles. They wouldn't be able to do that if they were working anywhere other than just outside the yard!
(Photo: P.Pescod Copyright www.transporttreasury.co.uk)

Left: The iconic Redbridge shunter was C14 class No.77s, built as No.745 at Eastleigh in 1907, it was transferred to Redbridge and re-numbered in October 1927 by the Southern. It is seen here at Redbridge in November 1928. Part of the old Linseed oil factory can be seen on the left.
(Photo: H.C.Casserley)

Right: When 77s was required back at Town Quay for shunting duties in 1957 among the locos to be used as substitutes were O2s. Here No. 30229 tries to squeeze into the loco shed, which was the old pump house, and was situated just by the down line to the west of the station, on 23rd April 1960. Beyond the shed to the right the 1883 viaduct over the river can be seen. On the left is the maintenance shop.
(Photo: James Harrold Copyright www.transporttreasury.co.uk)

Left: Engineering department stock could preserve some interesting items of rolling stock. Here Dick Riley photographed coach No.873S on 23rd May 1953. This was an ex-London Chatham and Dover Railway six-wheel carriage of 1894 and numbered 3630 by the Southern. It has been preserved and is now awaiting restoration at the Bluebell Railway.
(Photo: R.C.Riley Copyright www.transporttreasury.co.uk)

Right: By January 2011 all that is left of the Redbridge works site is this crane, preserved by the river side as a reminder of what was once here. The wharf-side area where the wood for the sleepers was unloaded is now a small park accessed by the footbridge at the station. Meanwhile the rest of the site is a giant car and van park for vehicles passing through the port.

Redbridge Causeway

Left: Standing on the by-pass bridge is a good vantage point to photograph trains crossing Redbridge Causeway heading to Totton. Here Maunsell Q class 0-6-0 No.30548 built in 1939, approaches the bridge with a train for Lymington Pier composed of pre-grouping stock on 17th May 1953.
(Photo: G.F.Bloxam Copyright P.F.Bloxam)

Right: BR Standard class 3 2-6-2 tank locomotive No.82015, built at Swindon in 1952, crosses Redbridge Causeway with a mixed goods train for Fawley on 5th May 1959.
(Photo: G.F.Bloxam Copyright P.F.Bloxam)

Left: U class Mogul No.31809 approaches the by-pass bridge with a Bournemouth train in August 1962. Things to note in this shot include the 1883 bridge, which the train has just crossed, the timber yard beside the Romsey line, and also Redbridge Towers being constructed in the background.
(Photo: A.J.Reeve Copyright Colour-Rail BRS1792)

Above: *Battle of Britain* class Pacific No.34058 *Sir Frederick Pile* is on a down stopping train to Bournemouth on 26th March 1964. On the left are the road works for the addition of a second carriageway to the by-pass, complete with new bridge over the mainline and the River Test. Unseen behind No.34058 and its train is the work in progress for the replacement of the 1883 viaduct. The locomotive is now preserved at the Mid-Hants Railway. (Photo: P.F.Bloxam)

Above: An identified *Voyager* class *Cross Country* train crosses the 1964-built Redbridge bridge heading into Redbridge on 18th January 2011.

Above: By crossing to the other side of the road on the by-pass bridge trains departing from Totton could be photographed. On 17th May 1953 Urie designed H15 class mixed traffic 4-6-0 locomotive No.30491, built by the LSWR in 1914 departs Totton with a London-line train. This seems to be made up of an interesting combination of passenger and parcels stock.

(Photo: G.F.Bloxam Copyright P.F.Bloxam)

Above: Now preserved as part of the National Collection Drummond designed T9 class 4-4-0 No.30120 departs from Totton with a train from Lymington Pier for Waterloo on 28th August 1954.

(Photo: G.F.Bloxam Copyright P.F.Bloxam)

Totton

Above: The guard poses for photos by the front buffers of Q1 class 0-6-0 No.33006 at the head of the LCGB's *New Forester* rail tour on 19th March 1966. This had just returned from the Fawley branch with USA locos Nos.30064 and 30073, and now 33006 had been attached to haul the train to Lymington and back to Brockenhurst.   (Photo: Copyright Colour-Rail 341951)

Most of the just over half-a-mile between Redbridge and Totton stations is spent crossing the viaduct over the River Test and associated causeway. Now the line passes under the flyover carrying the A35, originally built in 1930, over the line. In days past the next landmark would be the level crossing at the eastern end of Totton station.

Officially opened in 1859 the origins of Totton station seem to go back to almost the opening of the S&DR in 1847. Certainly in the *Hampshire Advertiser* in 1849 there is a reference to 'Eling Railway Station'. Timetables in the 1850s refer to some trains stopping 'at the signal at Eling Junction', and there is evidence that a short platform (or later platforms) existed by the Junction Road crossing to the west of the present station.

Not only that, but there also appears to have been station staff, as a newspaper report of 1856 refers to a stationmaster and porters. Therefore, this was an official stopping point, and was superseded by the building of Totton station, immediately adjacent to the level crossing where the main road to Lyndhurst crossed the line. It consisted of up and down platforms, with a single storey building on the up platform constructed of brick, and a wooden shelter on the down platform added soon afterwards. The platforms were lengthened in 1883.

By now the line to Beaulieu Road had been doubled, so there was no passing loop, and no signal box at the station until 1889. Then a disused box from Nursling was moved to the site to operate the crossing gates at a cost of £170. At the same time £430 was spent on a footbridge. A new down shelter with toilets was built in 1897.

To the west of the station was the junction for the Eling Tramway, which had been opened in 1851, curving away to the south. Here there was a trailing siding on the up side and two short sidings on the down. Two new sidings were laid on the up side later, one serving a loading dock, and the other to a flour mill in 1885.

Next came the Junction Road crossing, beside which stood Eling Junction signal box. This had been converted by the LSWR from an old crossing keeper's house and opened c1875. A footbridge was added here in 1896.

West of the Junction Road crossing on the south side was a wooden engine shed, which had been built in connection with the doubling of the line, and lasted until May 1895. This had originally housed the contractor's locomotive. It was here that the original platform (or platforms) was built.

Left: The station staff at Totton pose for this, turn of the 20th century, view from the station footbridge beside the old level crossing. The flour mill in the centre background is worth noting, which was served by a siding from the up line. In the distance Eling Junction signal box can be seen.
(Photo: Lens of Sutton Association)

Moving further towards Brockenhurst there was a large gravel pit, which was to supply the LSWR with ballast until the opening of Meldon Quarry. This became the site of the main goods yard in Totton in 1895 with three sidings and a goods shed connected to the down line. With the coming of the Fawley branch in 1925 a run-round loop was laid to the south of the goods yard, presumably to allow goods trains to reverse.

In the LSWR minutes the station, save for one year, is always known as Totton. In the timetables it was referred to as Totton for Eling, or Totton & Eling, which is how it is named in the 1866 timetable when six trains a day called in each direction. By 1876 there were seven passenger trains a day stopping there, one of which was mixed, and one goods train. Services improved and in 1909 seventeen down passenger trains called each week-day, two of which terminated at Totton. In 1918 it was reported that Totton was even making £1 a week selling platform tickets.

The Southern

The first major change under the SR was the opening of the branch to Fawley in July 1925. This led to extra facilities in the goods yard, already noted, plus additional trains calling at the station en-route between Southampton Terminus and Fawley.

During the later years of the 1920s the goods yard was a busy place, with annual tonnages of goods handled being 55,691 in 1928 and 69,116 in 1929, a significant part of which was fruit traffic. One unusual consignment handled at the yard was the Italian team's aircraft for the 1929 Schneider Trophy. The staff received a letter of appreciation from the team as a result.

In 1930 the A35 flyover was opened and the level crossing at the station was closed on 30th November. The signal box was later demolished.

Right: The down platform building at Totton, built in 1897, now demolished.
(Photo: Lens of Sutton Association)

Above: The scene in the goods yard at Totton where the Italian Schneider Trophy are either loading or unloading their planes for the competition in 1929.   (Photo: *Southern Railway Magazine* Copyright National Railway Museum/MMSI)

Train services were reduced during World War Two with only eleven down trains calling at the station in 1941, two of which were bound for Fawley and one for Lymington. The Totton area did not escape unscathed from the bombing, Eling wharf being hit in 1941. However, the only known railway casualty in the area was Totton goods clerk L.A.Smith, who was killed in a road traffic accident, while riding to work on his motorcycle in March 1945.

Nationalisation

Following the war the station was known simply as Totton in the 1947 timetable, when only eight trains called in the down direction, two bound for Fawley. In 1950 Eling Junction box was also renamed Totton.

As with other places, not much changed at the station during the 1950s. By 1964 twelve down trains called at the station each day, although the service could still be sporadic in the off-peak.

However, the 1960s saw significant changes. In January 1965 the up sidings were abolished. On 14th February 1966 passenger services were withdrawn from the Fawley branch. 1968 saw some of the down goods yard sidings east of the Junction road crossing lifted. A number of the sidings were removed from the west yard in 1970.

Of course 1967 saw the mainline electrified. Totton benefited from an improved service with hourly trains in each direction, slow to Bournemouth and semi-fast to

Left: The level crossing at Junction Road looking south on 28th August 1968. Originally the signal box was a crossing keeper's house and was extended c1875, when it was named Eling Junction. It was renamed Totton in 1950, and closed in 1982. To the right of this picture was probably original stopping point (station).
(Photo: K.G.Carr Copyright Peter Fidczuk)

Right: Looking towards Totton station from the Junction Road crossing footbridge. The old front door to the crossing keeper's house can clearly be seen at this end of the signal box. Meanwhile the branch to Eling wharf diverges from the down line just before the platform.

(Photo: K.G. Carr
Copyright Peter Fidczuk)

London. On 2nd April 1974 the 11.42am Waterloo to Bournemouth was routed onto the Fawley branch in error, coming to a stop beyond the conductor rail. It had to be pushed back onto the electrified section by a Fawley to Eastleigh freight.

Totton signal box was closed in 1982 and the crossing gates replaced by lifting barriers. Meanwhile the Eling Tramway finally closed in 1993, and the connection to the

down line was removed.

Today part of the west yard is still in use for engineers. Meanwhile the station is served by an hourly service in each direction between Poole and Waterloo operated by *South West Trains*. Passenger numbers are good with some 300,000 journeys starting or finishing at the station. A far cry from when trains simply stopped by the signal.

Above: Brush Type 4 No.D1926 passes the entrance to Totton yard as it approaches the station on the 9.40am Poole to Newcastle train on 20th May 1967. Note the double and single slips, as well as the ground frame building.

(Photo: John H.Bird Copyright SOUTHERN-Images)

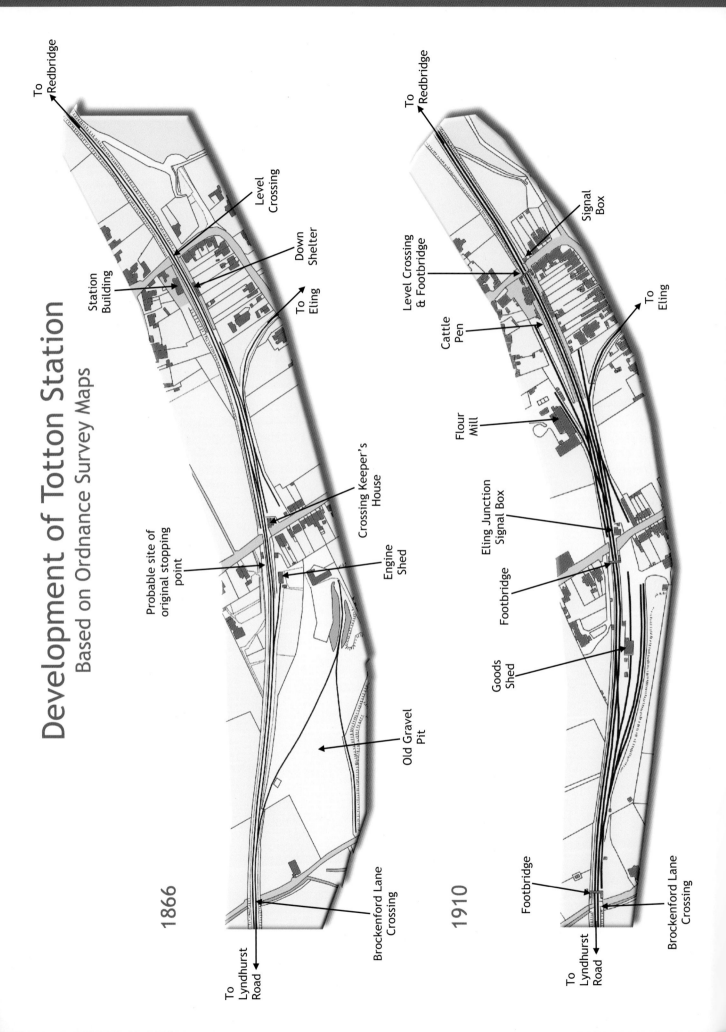

Development of Totton Station
Based on Ordnance Survey Maps

1866

To Redbridge

Level Crossing

Down Shelter

To Eling

Station Building

Crossing Keeper's House

Probable site of original stopping point

Engine Shed

Old Gravel Pit

Brockenford Lane Crossing

To Lyndhurst Road

1910

To Redbridge

Signal Box

Level Crossing & Footbridge

Cattle Pen

To Eling

Flour Mill

Eling Junction Signal Box

Footbridge

Goods Shed

Footbridge

To Lyndhurst Road

Brockenford Lane Crossing

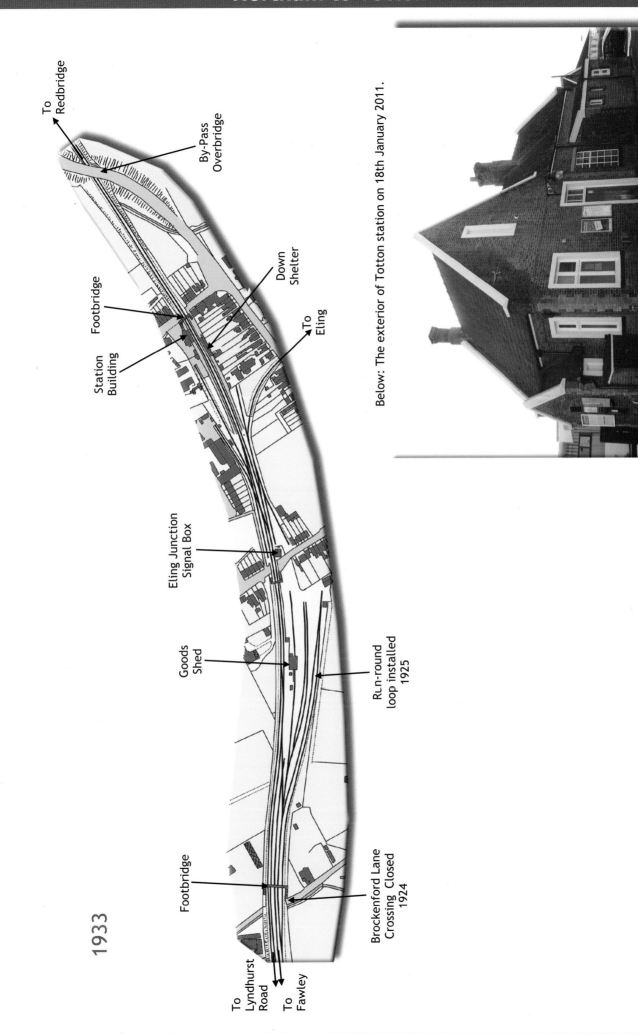

1933

To Redbridge

By-Pass Overbridge

Footbridge

Down Shelter

Station Building

To Eling

Eling Junction Signal Box

Goods Shed

Run-round loop installed 1925

Footbridge

Brockenford Lane Crossing Closed 1924

To Lyndhurst Road

To Fawley

Below: The exterior of Totton station on 18th January 2011.

Left: Another railtour at Totton, which has just returned from the Fawley branch on 9th April 1967. This time it is the LCGB *Hampshire Branch Lines* train which is standing at the station, while *USA* class locos Nos.30064 and 30069 are detached, and Standard class 4 tank No.80151, now preserved at the Bluebell Railway, is attached at the rear. The train then travelled to Lymington Pier.
(Photo: F.C.Hammersley)

Below: Totton station in the 1970s following the demolition of the down shelter.

The Southampton and Netley Railway

Above: A posed view of an ambulance train at Netley station. The connection between the clergy and railways is confirmed as the chaplain is one of those posing on the footplate of W.G.Beattie designed '302' class 0-6-0 No.336. This loco was originally built in 1876 and rebuilt by Adams in 1889. By the time of this photo it also sported a Drummond chimney. The ward cars behind are what were known as *Netley* cars converted from LSWR 48ft fruit vans in 1900. Their livery was khaki and french grey.

(Photo: Copyright Lens of Sutton Association)

As has been seen previously, the catalyst for moves to build a railway along the eastern shore of Southampton Water was the building of the great military hospital at Netley. Eventually the S&NR was built, opening between Portswood and Netley on 5th March 1866, having been absorbed by the LSWR in January 1865.

There were two substantial engineering works on the line, the bridge over the River Itchen and a viaduct at Miller's Pond near Sholing. Otherwise this opened as a country branch line with stations at Bitterne Road, Woolston and Netley along its 4.85 mile length. A few months later a station was opened at Sholing. Early train services consisted of eight return trains on weekdays and three on Sundays.

Although the opening day trains were reported to have been well filled, traffic in those early days was not spectacular, and by 1877 the service was still the same. One train plied between Southampton Docks and Netley, starting from Southampton at 7.35am, with the last train returning there at 9.08pm.

Connection to Fareham

It was of course logical that an extension be made to link Netley to the Portsmouth line at Fareham, and make a direct rail connection between Southampton and Portsmouth. Certainly the military authorities saw the merit of this and encouraged schemes to be developed.

The full story of these proposals will be dealt with in a later volume, but in 1882 the LSWR decided to promote a route linking Netley and Fareham via Hamble, Bursledon and Swanwick. Thought was also given to doubling the line at this time but was rejected. However, the railway opened through to Fareham on 2nd September 1889, and so Netley ceased being a terminus station.

By 1896 through trains were operating between Portsmouth and Cardiff, and passenger services had increased to seventeen passenger trains in each direction each day, along with two goods trains by 1909. This was a measure of the increased traffic the new connection to Fareham had made.

Left: M7 No.30357 0-4-4 tank arrives at Netley with a Portsmouth train in 1957, although the loco bears a pre-1956 BR totem.
(Photo: N. Hamshire Copyright Kidderminster Railway Museum)

Connections to Netley Hospital

It is interesting that while the hospital was very much the main *raison d'être* for the line to Netley, it would not be until 1900 that the hospital was directly connected to the railway. This, apparently, only occurred after some pressure from Queen Victoria. Instead for many years a platform was provided in the goods yard at Netley for the use of patients travelling to the hospital. The hospital branch remained in use until December 1963, although it had been dormant for some years.

Further Developments under the LSWR

In 1906 a there was a deputation from the Itchen Urban District Council to the LSWR requesting that a steam railmotor be introduced on the line, with a new halt at Keepers' Bottom, and a goods siding built at Sholing. In the end nothing came of any of these requests.

Another possible development came in 1909 when it was proposed to build a new graving dock on the eastern shore of the River Itchen. This would have been served by a one and a half mile line curving round in a horseshoe shape from a junction half a mile beyond Sholing. Again nothing came of this. However, in November 1909 doubling of the line was authorised.

Doubling proceeded in stages along the route, between St Denys and Bitterne it was completed on 27th February 1910, between Bitterne and Woolston on 10th April, and finally between Woolston and Netley on 29th May 1910. But it was to be nearly another year before all the line to Fareham was so treated, the final section not coming into use until 9th April 1911. Meanwhile other through trains between Bournemouth and Portsmouth, Plymouth and Portsmouth, Cardiff and Brighton, Plymouth and Brighton, and Bradford-on-Avon to Portsmouth were introduced that made use of the route.

World War One of course saw heavy use of the line to and from the hospital for ambulance trains. In addition there were also extra trains to Netley for construction workers engaged in building an airfield at Hamble.

Grouping and Beyond

During the time the line was under the SR relatively little seems to have changed. However, due to the expansion of the suburbs of Bitterne, Woolston and Sholing, which were not served by the trams, passenger numbers increased significantly.

By 1935 services consisted of a mix of predominantly local services to Portsmouth originating at Southampton Terminus, Eastleigh (via Southampton), Andover, Salisbury and Millbrook (Brockenhurst on Saturdays). In addition to the previously mentioned express services, there was also a through service between Bournemouth and Guildford.

The Second World War brought increased traffic to the line with the movement of service personnel to and from Southampton docks and Portsmouth, particularly with the departure of troops in 1939, the evacuation from Dunkirk, and D-Day. Of course too there were services to Netley Hospital, although casualties were usually brought to the hospital by road,and shipped out by rail.

Services had recovered by 1947. Now there were 21 down services a day using the line, again predominately local services to and from Portsmouth. In 1954, under the auspices of British Railways, there were 52 train movements on the line every weekday. These included goods workings to and from Bitterne, Fareham and Woolston, and various through trains. 1954 also saw the establishment of Woolston Tip and associated sidings between Woolston and Bitterne, served by regular trains of rubbish.

Most local trains in the post-war period were worked by locomotives such as the T9, D15, L12, S11, & L11 classes, all 4-4-0 tender locomotives of pre-grouping origin. Through trains were in the hands of N or U class 2-6-0 Moguls, or GWR *Halls*. Again the carriage stock was mainly pre-grouping LSWR compartment stock, although later LSWR and Maunsell corridor coaches were observed on the line.

Goods services were withdrawn from Bitterne in 1959; Netley in 1962 and Woolston yard in 1966. However, services to and from Woolston Tip continued until June 1976.

The introduction of the *Hampshire* DEMUs in 1957 brought a major timetable revision with most trains being speeded up. Train services in 1964 consisted of hourly slow and semi-fast services in both directions.

There were also through trains from Brighton to Plymouth, three from Portsmouth to Cardiff and return, and one from Portsmouth to Plymouth. The Plymouth trains were mainly handled by *West Country* or *Battle of Britain* class locomotives.

After the end of steam slowly the numbers of through trains diminished, until in 1972 the only regular through trains ran between Cardiff or Bristol and Portsmouth. These used loco-hauled mark 1 stock, with a Saturdays only train between Brighton and Exeter, made up of *Hastings* units. However, by 1982 the number of through workings between Cardiff and Bristol to Portsmouth had increased to ten.

Electrification and Privatisation

In 1972 there was a government leak that the whole future of the line was under review. Happily this proved to be a false alarm, and, as has been seen, in fact services on the line began to increase. In addition colour light signalling and block working were introduced in March 1980 with the signal boxes at Netley and Woolston closed (Bitterne had already closed in 1966). The box at Adelaide crossing survived until October 1981 when it too closed, operations now being controlled from Eastleigh.

DMU *Sprinters* from classes 155, 156 and 158 were introduced from the late 1980s. These were quickly superceded between Southampton and Portsmouth, when the line between St Denys and Fareham was electrified in May 1990. Diesel units still operate the services that use the non-electrified routes to Romsey, Salisbury, Bristol and Cardiff.

Under Privatisation, trains from three different companies use the route. *South West Trains* operates hourly local services between Portsmouth and Southampton with *Desiro* units. *Southern* operates regular electric through services to Brighton, Gatwick and London Victoria, with class 377 *Electrostar* units, while *First Great Western* utilises diesel units between Cardiff and Portsmouth (usually class 158s).

Today the line probably sees its most intensive passenger service since opening, with at least three trains an hour passing in each direction for most of the day. Certainly there seems to be no threat to the line for the foreseeable future.

Above: Unrebuilt *West Country* No. 34007 *Wadebridge* passes Woolston on the 3.28pm Fareham to Stanlow oil tank train on 24th August 1965. The goods yard is still open at this time.

(Photo: John H.Bird Copyright SOUTHERN-images)

Route of the former S&NR
Based on Ordnance Survey Map of 1945

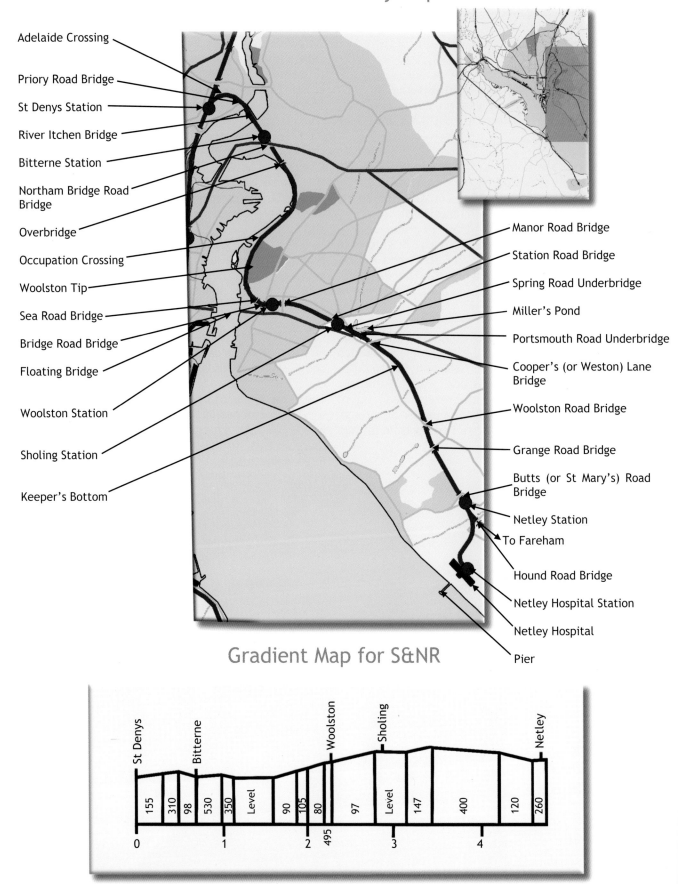

Adelaide Crossing

Priory Road Bridge

St Denys Station

River Itchen Bridge

Bitterne Station

Northam Bridge Road Bridge

Overbridge

Occupation Crossing

Woolston Tip

Sea Road Bridge

Bridge Road Bridge

Floating Bridge

Woolston Station

Sholing Station

Keeper's Bottom

Manor Road Bridge

Station Road Bridge

Spring Road Underbridge

Miller's Pond

Portsmouth Road Underbridge

Cooper's (or Weston) Lane Bridge

Woolston Road Bridge

Grange Road Bridge

Butts (or St Mary's) Road Bridge

Netley Station

To Fareham

Hound Road Bridge

Netley Hospital Station

Netley Hospital

Pier

Gradient Map for S&NR

St Denys — Bitterne — Woolston — Sholing — Netley

| 155 | 310 | 98 | 530 | 350 | Level | 90 | 105 | 80 | 97 | Level | 147 | 400 | 120 | 260 |

495

0   1   2   3   4

Mileage from St Denys
Ordinants in form 1 in x

Right: Cheap Southern Railway fares available from the Southampton area in 1936.

Right: Arriving at platform four at St Denys on the tight curve is BR Standard class 5 mixed traffic locomotive No.73170, with a train from Waterloo for Southampton docks via Eastleigh and Fareham on 25th April 1965. This was presumably due to engineering work on the mainline.

(Photo: P.Pescod Copyright transporttreasury.co.uk)

Views of Adelaide Crossing.

Left: Looking north up Adelaide Road probably just a few years after the signal box was erected in 1899.
(Photo: Lens of Sutton Association)

Below Right: Adelaide Crossing box in 1974, now with half-barriers installed on the crossing.

Below Left: Inside Adelaide Crossing box in 1980.
(Photo: G.Wheeler)

Bitterne

Above: For the second time in these pages T9 No.30120 appears, this time pulling into Bitterne with a Brockenhurst to Portsmouth & Southsea service on 2nd October 1957. The station building on the right is original, the signal box probably erected in 1889, while the corrugated iron hut was built in 1903. (Photo: C.Saunders Copyright R.K.Blencowe collection)

The history of St Denys station was set out in the section on the line between Terminus and Airport, and so will not be dealt with here. Instead our journey along the line to Netley starts as a train departs from platform three at St Denys.

At this point the line is on a curve, which tightens to 275yd radius beyond the station. After just a few yards the train crosses Adelaide Road on a crossing that, up to 11th October 1981, was controlled by Adelaide Crossing signal box which stood on the north side of the line. This box was a smaller version of St Denys box on the London line. It was constructed when the station was rebuilt in 1899 and served as a block post for the single section to Bitterne until the line was doubled in 1910. Then it reverted to simply controlling the crossing and associated signals until it was closed with Eastleigh taking over operations in 1981. On the crossing itself barriers replaced the gates in June 1966.

Rising now on a gradient of 1 in 155, the line crosses Priory Road on a low single 30ft span girder bridge before coming to the western shore of the Itchen and crossing the river bridge. This was built on cast iron piles sunk 60ft below the surface of the Itchen, with three spans each 36yds long, and cost in the region of £15,000 to construct. It was built to be 20ft above the river at high tide, and was lit with gas lights to aid the navigation of barges through it.

Beyond the bridge the original course of the route would have climbed Lance's Hill on a grade of 1 in 90. However, the line that was built now falls at 1 in 98, past the site

of the former Roman settlement at Clausentum and Bitterne Manor on the right, before coming to Bitterne Road station three-quarters of a mile from St Denys.

Bitterne Road (later Bitterne) station was built just as the line crossed under the Northam Bridge Road at the foot of Lance's Hill. It was originally going to be called Northam Road for Bitterne, but opened with the name Bitterne Road on 5th March 1866. The original station was a 'modest structure' with a single platform and building, there was even talk that the building would be a 'moveable iron house', in other words, corrugated iron. However, something more substantial was provided but not on the scale of the stations at St Denys, Woolston or Netley.

Some debate has taken place over the years about the provision of crossing places on the Netley line. However, it is clear that Bitterne was not provided with a crossing loop at first. But a loop was built when the line between Fareham and Netley opened in 1889, when the up platform, and signal box were added at a cost of £1,154. Meanwhile in 1873 a siding for coal traffic was laid, at

London and South Western Ry.
787
From WATERLOO
TO
Bitterne Road

Left: This photo quite probably is pre-1910 when the line was doubled, as the signalman is apparently collecting the single line token from the fireman. The locomotive is an 0-6-0, No.29, of the Adams-designed '395' class, which appears to be hauling a mixed goods train. This locomotive was built in 1885, and lasted in service until 1958. On the up platform the waiting shelter can be seen.
(Photo: Lens of Sutton collection)

the north end of what became the down platform, with a further siding added in 1883.

In November 1896 the station was renamed Bitterne, and in 1902 it is recorded that the waiting shelter on the up platform was enlarged. More land was also acquired for the goods yard and a new rooms added to the stationmaster's residence. A footbridge was provided in 1903, and a corrugated iron store in 1905.

As has been previously stated the line through Bitterne was doubled in stages through 1910, and an additional siding laid in the goods yard. Alterations were also made to the road bridge at this time.

Southern and British Railways

Like much of this line, little changed at Bitterne during the time of the Southern. Staff came and went. Mr. Gaiger who had been stationmaster since May 1916 retired at the end of 1928, when the station came under the stationmaster at Woolston, but in 1936 it regained its own stationmaster, Mr. R.J. Hookey.

In September 1930 there was concern about the state of the

road bridge. A 5mph speed restriction was imposed on the bridge by Southampton Corporation, and only one bus at a time was allowed to cross it until it was rebuilt. This seems to have happened shortly afterwards.

Bitterne station does not seem to have suffered significantly as a result of the Second World War, and it entered Nationalisation in much the same state as it was absorbed by the SR in 1923. On 13th July 1959 goods services were withdrawn, with the yard being taken out of use on 29th August 1961, and the track being lifted the following year. Then on 10th October 1966 the signal box was closed, being demolished three years later.

However, there were improvements, and in 1968 passengers had the benefit of electric lighting on the platforms. With electrification in 1990 new waiting shelters were also provided. In recent years there has been a growth in the passenger numbers, and in 2009-10 it is estimated that some 69,454 journeys started or concluded at the station.

Right: An early 20th century view of Bitterne station. By this time the old coach body which acted as a goods store (seen on page 17) had been removed, a new goods store having been constructed in 1905.
(Commercial Postcard)

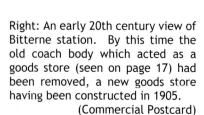

Left: A view of the station from the St Denys end looking towards the road bridge taken on 5th August 1964. (Photo: K.G.Carr Copyright P.Fidczuk)

Above: A reminder that locomotives did work tender-first, as Q1 class No 33009 rumbles through Bitterne with a train of tank wagons from Hamble to North Camp, on 9th April 1965. (Photo: John H. Bird Copyright SOUTHERN-images)

Above: Bitterne station buildings on 24th November 2010.

Above: Bitterne station from the road bridge on 24th November 2010. Note the extra supports for the footbridge.

Development of Bitterne Station
Based on Ordnance Survey Maps

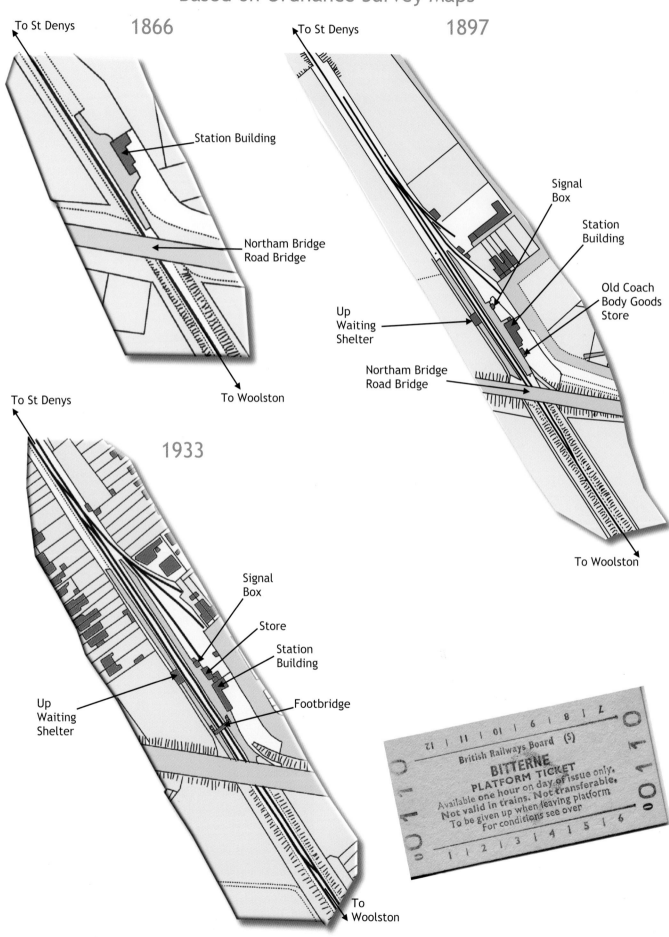

1866

To St Denys

Station Building

Northam Bridge
Road Bridge

To Woolston

1897

To St Denys

Signal
Box

Station
Building

Old Coach
Body Goods
Store

Up
Waiting
Shelter

Northam Bridge
Road Bridge

To Woolston

1933

To St Denys

Signal
Box

Store

Station
Building

Footbridge

Up
Waiting
Shelter

To
Woolston

British Railways Board (S)

BITTERNE
PLATFORM TICKET
Available one hour on day of issue only.
Not valid in trains. Not transferable.
To be given up when leaving platform
For conditions see over

Left: *Hampshire* DEMU No.1105 is seen from the Northam Road Bridge on the approach to Bitterne with a train from Portsmouth for Andover Junction on 5th August 1964. In the background is an occupation bridge.
(Photo: K.G.Carr collection Copyright Peter Fidczuk)

Right: 2-6-0 BR Standard class 4 No.76017 passes along the river's edge on its way from Woolston to Bitterne on 12th July 1956 with a train for Salisbury from Portsmouth Harbour. No.76017 is preserved at the Mid-Hants Railway.
(Photo: D. Cull Copyright Kidderminster Railway Museum)

Left: U class Mogul No.31794 with a train for Portsmouth on the shoreline between Bitterne and Woolston in September 1954.
(Photo: Copyright Colour-Rail 342188)

Woolston Tip

Right: Class 33 No.33001 at Woolston Tip preparing for the last departure on 10th June 1976. Some local youngsters are climbing on the CCT vehicle behind.
(Photo: R.Newman)

Left: No.33001 prepares to leave with the last train of empty wagons, while a down 2-car *Hampshire* DEMU has passed by on the down line to Woolston. In the background construction work is well advanced on the new Itchen bridge, which would replace the floating bridge.
(Photo: R.Newman)

Right: The ground frame at Woolston Tip sidings. This was released from Woolston signal box, and worked in conjunction with the signalman at Woolston.
(Photo: R.Newman)

Woolston

Above: Unrebuilt *Battle of Brtain* class No.34066 *Spitfire* rounds the curve on the approach to Woolston station in 1965. This locomotive was involved in the Lewisham accident in 1957, but had been repaired and put back into service.

(Photo: Copyright Colour-Rail BRS505)

Departing from Bitterne the train passes under the Northam Bridge Road and through a cutting under an occupation bridge. Emerging from the cutting it follows the shoreline of the east bank of the Itchen. Curving south west on an embankment it then comes to an occupation crossing which served a yacht and ship-building yard.

Along this stretch of line in April 1934 a train was derailed by stones on the line. Four boys appeared in court charged with trespass. One, a nine year old, was found guilty of actually putting the stones on the rails and his father was fined £2.

Now the line begins to climb on an embankment with gradients between 1 in 80 and 1 in 105, and passing over a bridge as it does so. To the right are the shipyards and the river, while to the left is Peartree Green.

It is here that a rubbish tip was established in 1954 on the down side of the line to fill in a deep gully, with series of sidings, operated by a ground frame, being brought into use the same year. The tip remained in use until June 1976. Between 1960 and 1971 its operation was undertaken by a private contractor who employed diesel shunters to move wagons on the temporary tracks.

Passing over a bridge across Sea Road (previously High Street) the track now continues to climb and turns east passing through a cutting and under a footbridge as it does so. It now crosses Bridge Road and enters Woolston station on a curve with a 20mph speed restriction in steam days, having travelled one and a quarter miles from Bitterne.

Woolston Station

Woolston station was built at the insistence of the Itchen Bridge Company, to permit people to disembark from the train and travel across to Southampton by the floating bridge. However, in truth Woolston was also an ideal spot to build a station, as it was mid-way between St Denys and Netley and had an established population. Therefore, the station was a grand affair, the main station building a copy of the building at St Denys, only covered with stucco. The similarity in the style of the buildings at St Denys, Woolston and Netley to that at Terminus has led to the speculation that they were designed by a partner

London and South Western Ry.
787
TO
WOOLSTON

Left: Adams designed class '135' 4-4-0 No.139 arrives at Woolston in the early years of the 20th century with a train for Portsmouth from Salisbury. This loco was built in December 1880, and lasted in service until 1924. By now the station had a loop and signal box. Note also the footbridge and also the station bookstall under the canopy.

(Photo: Lens of Sutton Association)

in William Tite's firm, E.N. Clifton.

Again we return to the subject of crossing loops. There seems no doubt that Woolston was originally built with two platforms, the main station building on the up platform, and a waiting room on the down, with a loop and single siding. However, there is no indication of a signal box at this time. Therefore, it is possible that the loop was built for the use of goods traffic, or in the expectation that increased passenger services would be required with an extension to Fareham.

In the event until the Fareham extension opened passenger services were operated by a single coaching set plying between Netley and Docks stations. When the Fareham line opened, however, it seems as if the passing places were established at Bitterne, Netley and Swanwick. The logic behind this was that there is approximately four miles between each of these locations, and also between Swanwick and Fareham. Also Bitterne, as I think Bert Moody rightly speculates, was chosen so that trains could cross or be held there, in order to

avoid congestion at the then limited facilities at St Denys.

However, there was a loop at Woolston in 1876 when one goods train a day terminated there. Then in 1879 the LSWR minutes stated that the loop line was to be altered, which led to the arrangement seen in the Ordnance Survey plan of 1897. There was, though, a run-round facility available by an extra connection into the goods yard.

Meanwhile, additional sidings had been provided in 1877 and 1882, with a crane added in 1877. A short headshunt was also laid in 1880. Intriguingly in 1884 it seems as if the old loop, now a siding, was extended westwards into what was described as a private 'ballast field'.

But by 1901 the loop was re-instated and a signal box built to the same style as that at Adelaide crossing, enabling the station to become a crossing point on the line. A

Right: The up platform at Woolston station in the early years of the 20th century after the signal box had been built.

(Photo: Lens of Sutton Association)

Above: Aftermath of a bombing at Woolston. The goods office and down waiting room have been damaged, while men are working on the signal and the telegraph lines.

(Photo: Courtesy *Southern Daily Echo*)

footbridge was also provided and a small extension made to the down waiting room all costing £2,949. Of course all these loops were rendered redundant when the line was doubled in 1910.

During 1910 the headshunt was extended until it reached some 470 yards from the signal box. Here a ground frame operated the connection to the down line on the newly doubled line to Netley. In addition, a wooden goods office appeared next to the Bridge Road overbridge.

In 1907 further land was purchased to allow for the expansion of the goods yard, and, around the time of doubling, a large goods shed seems to have been built. The presence of nearby shipbuilder *J.I.Thornycroft & Co*, meant a good deal of goods traffic came through Woolston yard, but there were also several coal merchants based on the site.

Grouping

As elsewhere on the line Grouping seems to have made little difference to Woolston, and life continued until the Second World War. However, the presence of the major engineering sites on the Itchen such as the *Supermarine* works, meant that Woolston yard became busy, with a new electric crane installed. However, this also meant that the area was a prime candidate for attack from German bombers.

There was a heavy raid on 24th November 1940, which

Right: Woolston station building and signal box on 7th March 1980, just after the latter had been closed. It can be clearly seen that the box was to the same design as that at Adelaide crossing.

(Photo: R.Newman)

Left: The down shelter in 1974. Note the extension to the original 1866 building.

resulted in a train being hit by a bomb near Woolston station destroying a coach and killing one person. At around the same time, a bridge at Woolston was damaged and a repair crew from Fratton was sent out to clear the line. Unfortunately, German bombers made a daylight raid on the area and three of the crew were killed.

Nationalisation

With the end of the war and Nationalisation there was an increase in services and traffic. It was reported that for four weeks in March 1949 cartage from the station had amounted to 1,279 tons of goods, a record since the service was introduced in May 1940.

There were also times for celebration, such as the decoration of the station in July 1957 for the local carnival. A train carried the carnival king and queen all the way from Sholing for the occasion!

However, the 1960s brought decline to the station. In March 1966 the goods yard was closed to general traffic, and to coal traffic in the October, although the coal merchants continued to use the

yard until it was cleared of traders in 1985. By the end of January 1968 all the sidings were taken out of use, although on a happier note electric lighting was installed on the platforms the same year.

Later with the commissioning of colour light signalling the signal box was closed in March 1980, and the goods shed demolished in 1986. Since then housing has been built over the former goods yard coming right up to the down platform. In 1990 the line was electrified and a new booking office was opened in the station building, while the majority of the building was let for office use.

In 2011 outside the main station building the road now runs on to the new Itchen bridge, while the down side has a 'hemmed in' feel because of the housing. The signal box is currently boarded up, having served as a clubroom for the Solent Model Railway Group for many years. They have now moved their base to St Denys. However, Woolston is still well used with an estimated 125,296 passenger journeys starting or finishing there in 2009-10, and there is still something of the elegance it had when built nearly 150 years ago.

Right: Although the goods yard was closed and the tracks lifted, the goods shed was still in use in 1974 as a base for a firm of hauliers.

Woolston Station Through The Years

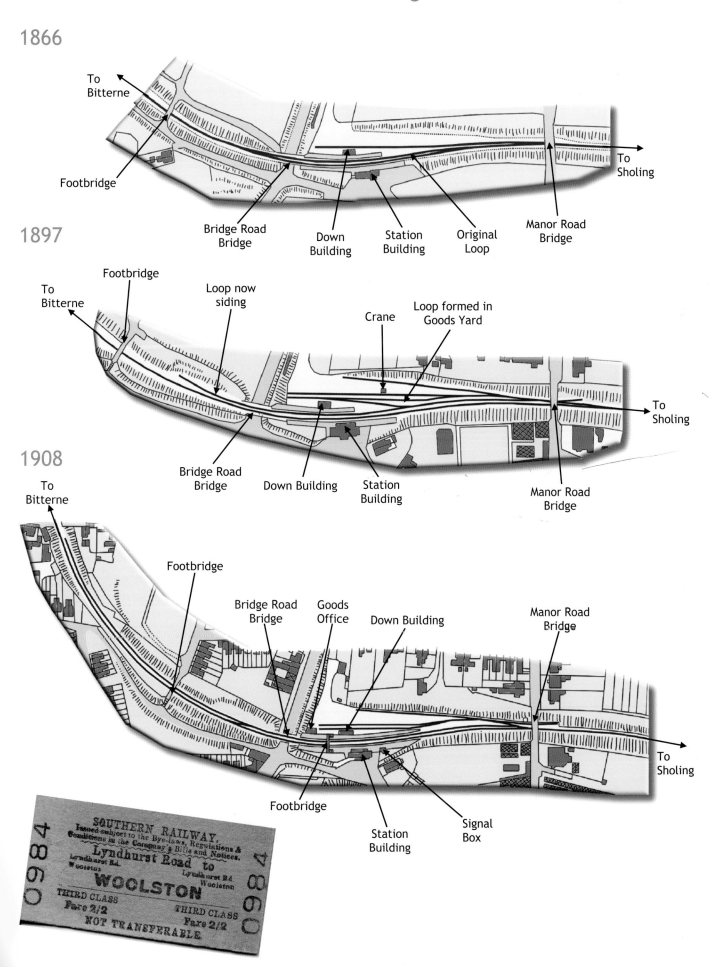

1866

To Bitterne

Footbridge

Bridge Road Bridge

Down Building

Station Building

Original Loop

Manor Road Bridge

To Sholing

1897

Footbridge

To Bitterne

Loop now siding

Crane

Loop formed in Goods Yard

To Sholing

Bridge Road Bridge

Down Building

Station Building

Manor Road Bridge

1908

To Bitterne

Footbridge

Bridge Road Bridge

Goods Office

Down Building

Manor Road Bridge

To Sholing

Footbridge

Station Building

Signal Box

SOUTHERN RAILWAY.
Issued subject to the Bye-laws, Regulations &
Conditions in the Company's Bills and Notices.
Lyndhurst Road to
Lyndhurst Rd.
Woolston
Lyndhurst Rd.
Woolston
WOOLSTON
THIRD CLASS
Fare 2/2
THIRD CLASS
Fare 2/2
NOT TRANSFERABLE

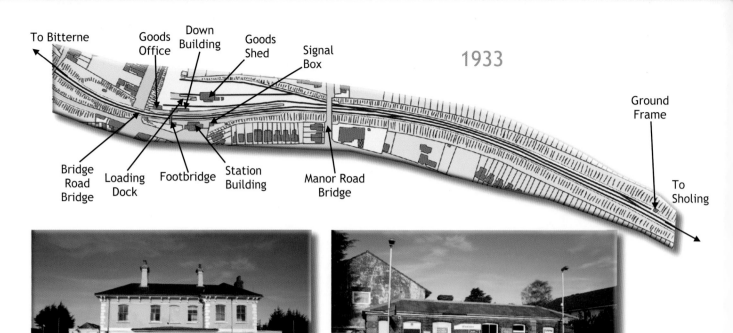

To Bitterne

Goods Office

Down Building

Goods Shed

Signal Box

1933

Ground Frame

To Sholing

Bridge Road Bridge

Loading Dock

Footbridge

Station Building

Manor Road Bridge

Woolston station building in November 2010. It is worth comparing the building to that at St Denys on page 58 to see the similarity.

The down side building at Woolston, now hemmed in by housing, in November 2010.

The Floating Bridge

Floating bridges were invented by James Rendel, with the first example entering service at Dartmouth in 1832. The floating bridge at Southampton was the third to be developed, and was opened by the *Itchen Bridge Company* on 23rd November 1836 between Southampton and Woolston.

Initially it struggled with competition from the Northam Bridge, and also the fact that Woolston was little more than a fishing village. The company was bankrupted twice in 1839 and 1849, with the service not operating between 1850 and 1852.

In the event the company was reformed, and, with the building of the Netley Hospital, trade picked up. However, with its marginal existence it can be understood why the development of the S&NR was viewed with concern. But traffic increased and a second set of chains was added in 1881.

In 1929 Southampton Corporation took over Northam Bridge which became free, with a resulting loss in trade to the floating bridge. Therefore, the Company sold the bridge to the Corporation in September 1934.

The first diesel powered bridge entered service in 1962, and in 1967 the last steam bridge was scrapped. Construction of the fixed Itchen Bridge began in 1974, and on 11th June 1977 the last crossing took place.

Left: The last steam bridge, No.10 built by *Day, Summers, & Co. Ltd.* of Northam in 1928 is seen during its final period of operation in the summer of 1966. (Photo: T.Hastings)

Sholing

Above: On 12th June 1965 BR Standard class 4 No.75070 passes through Sholing with a RCTS special.

(Photo: L.E.Elsey Copyright Colour-Rail 381411)

From Woolston to Sholing is a short run of about six-tenths of a mile on a continuous grade of 1 in 97 through a cutting. During this time the route passes under Manor Road overbridge before curving south east and then continues straight under Station Road bridge and into Sholing station.

Sholing is not one of the original stations on the line, but was opened shortly afterwards, the LSWR responding to local representations. As a result in May 1866 it was decided to open a 'temporary wooden box and platform' as 'an experiment', which came into use in August 1866. Initially named Scholing it had a small wooden station building and signal box along with its single platform. Sholing never had a loop or any sidings, despite requests for the latter.

However, traffic at the station was low, as in May 1869 it was decided to close the station from 1st July. This does not seem to have happened, and 1875 an estimate of £650 was prepared for providing a new station. Quite what was provided at this point, if anything, is unclear. Some excitement did occur in 1881 when someone broke into the 'counting house' at the station and stole a coat.

More work seems to have been carried out at the station in the mid 1890s, because in December 1895 there is a newspaper report of the inquest into a man killed on the line at Sholing. The man was said to be a bricklayer engaged in building a structure to replace the existing station, and was killed as he headed home from his work by a fast train from Netley. Certainly a new station building seems to have been constructed around this time.

In 1910 the station had to be rebuilt again to allow the line to be doubled, with the existing structures being demolished, and new platforms with buildings provided on the up and down sides. The down platform was linked by a ramp to the existing road bridge, and a footbridge provided between the two platforms. A few months after

London and South Western Ry.

787

From WATERLOO

TO

SHOLING

Above: Sholing station at the beginning of the 20th century before the line was doubled. The old coach body is worth noting, certainly of a later vintage to those seen at Swaythling and Bitterne, and also the fine rack of fire buckets. The house to be seen over the bridge was the stationmaster's residence. (Photo: B. Moody collection)

the new station opened the platforms were extended to their present length.

The SR maintained this small station, but sought to make savings. It seems that the last stationmaster at Sholing was a Mr. Reed who retired at the end of October 1926. Thereafter the station came under the jurisdiction of the stationmaster at Woolston. Parcels and other small goods traffic stopped being dealt with at the station in July 1932.

Sholing survived virtually unaltered into the days of British Railways becoming an unstaffed halt in December

1965. Between 1967 and 1985 the Southampton Model Railway Club had their clubroom in the former down building. However, as part of the electrification scheme the old buildings were demolished and replaced by waiting shelters on the up and down lines in 1990.

Today Sholing is still well used, and indeed has seen substantial increases in its passenger numbers. Between 2007-08 and 2009-10 estimated passenger journeys starting or finishing at Sholing increased from 46,523 to 70,744. Therefore, the future seems good for this small station, on what was originally a country branch line.

Left: A train enters Sholing station probably in the early 1900s before the line was doubled. It is worth noting that the bridge was built for double track, and also the signal to the left of the locomotive. The onlookers were quite possibly 'added in' to the scene.
(Photo: Courtesy *Southern Daily Echo*)

The Development of Sholing

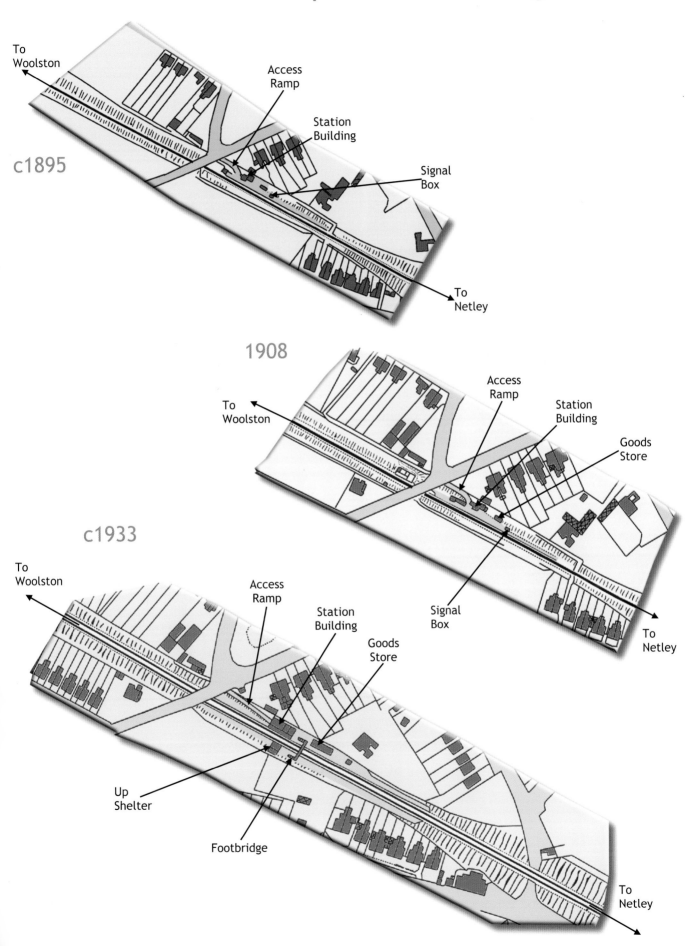

c1895

To Woolston

Access Ramp

Station Building

Signal Box

To Netley

1908

To Woolston

Access Ramp

Station Building

Goods Store

Signal Box

To Netley

c1933

To Woolston

Access Ramp

Station Building

Goods Store

Up Shelter

Footbridge

To Netley

Left: Conversation at Sholing with a discussion going on with the driver of the *Hampshire* unit standing at the up platform heading for Southampton probably in the early 1960s. Note that the booking office is open, while the station building boasts a fine array of chimneys.

(Photographer Unknown)

Right: On 28th March 1965 the buildings on the down platform, particularly the goods store and office, are photographed from an up train. This building also contained the porters' room.
(Photo: Copyright HMRS J.J.Davis collection)

Left: Sholing station from the Netley end in April 1975. The buildings had recently been renovated. On the extreme right is the remains of a concrete telegraph pole.
(Photo: R.Newman)

Right: From Station Road bridge in March 2011. The old buildings have been swept away, but the footbridge remains.

Netley

Above: Nearly at the end of steam on Southern Region BR Standard class 4 No. 76067 approaches Netley with an up parcels train in May 1967 passing the remains of the goods yard and hospital branch. (Photo John H.Bird Copyright SOUTHERN-images)

After Sholing the line crosses two bridges at Miller's Pond the first of which is a single girder bridge over Spring Road, while the second is a three arch brick-built viaduct. This is the second biggest engineering structure on the run to Netley, which carries the railway over the Portsmouth Road. From here there is a climb of 1 in 147 through a cutting and under the Weston Lane overbridge.

Now the summit is reached, and beyond is the point where the line to the new graving dock would have diverged to the right. Moving south east there is an occupation crossing, which would have been the site of the requested halt at Keeper's Bottom. From here the gradient is downhill at 1 in 400 passing under Woolston Road and Grange Road bridges. At this point the train rounds a 330 yard radius curve and passes under the Butts Road (or St Mary's Road after c1960) overbridge and into Netley station. This, up until 1889, was the end of the line.

It was on this stretch of track on 15th September 1879 that the 1.55pm Southampton to Netley train, hauled by a Beattie designed *Nelson* class 2-4-0 well-tank locomotive, ran through the station and into four loaded wagons at the buffer stops just over 300yds beyond the platform. The train consisted of five coaches, one 1st, a 2nd, two third and a 'break' van. One passenger and the fireman were injured, and the cause was put down to the driver not applying the brakes early enough.

A Terminus

During its life Netley has been a terminus, a through station and a junction. Originally it was a simple terminus with a larger station building than St Denys or Woolston, again in the *Italianate* style and covered with stucco. It possessed a run round loop and two platforms, although in the early days only the up platform was used. It is possible that two platforms were provided, because originally it was envisaged that there would be a rapid extension on towards Fareham, but the financial crash of the mid 1860s meant that any such plans were put on hold.

There was a short siding to a loading dock at the northern end of the up platform, while beyond the platforms there was a siding on the up side of the line, where a crane was provided a few months after the line opened. Another siding led to a turntable on the down side. At the end of the line by the buffer stops a loading dock was built for coal wagons in 1867. It is possible that this was used for

the early transfer of patients to and from Netley Hospital. Later there is a record of a platform being erected at the station in 1869 for this purpose, but the minutes state that there would be no shelter unless the War Office paid. The presence of the turntable indicated that tender locomotives were used on the line, and indeed accounts relate that they were used to haul the trains on the opening day.

Traffic appears to have been steady rather than spectacular. However, on 25th June 1877 a major temperance rally was held at Netley Abbey and it is recorded that many people were transported there on special trains including workers from the *Huntley & Palmer* biscuit factory at Reading. Queen Victoria also used the station on a number of occasions to visit the hospital, once on 29th November 1882, and no fewer than three times in 1898. She even made a final visit in May 1900 to open the new hospital branch, which will be recorded later.

Over the years the facilities were developed. A signal box seems to have been added in the 1870s, which was later extended, probably when the Fareham line opened. Gas was provided at the station in 1873. In 1884 additional sidings were laid in the goods yard, and the loading dock extended. Work on the new line between Netley and Fareham began in 1886, which was to turn Netley into a through station.

Left: Station staff at Netley probably around 1906. In this photograph two members of staff can be identified, both of whom appear in the lower photograph. Standing in the centre in the top photograph, and perched on the trolley in the lower one is Mr.J.W.Sedgewick, described as head porter in the lower photograph. Meanwhile, seated at the left-hand end of the bench in the top photograph and standing at the foot of the steps in the lower picture is Mr.W.Selby, porter.

Right: Identified in this photograph taken c1910, in addition to those mentioned above, are Mr.H.Davis, signalman, standing on the signal box steps, while standing by the entrance there is Mr.F.Russel, porter-signalman and on the right Mr.F.Fagant porter-signalman. Leaning up against the steps in the centre is the stationmaster Mr.G.R.Goss to his left is Mr.Lance, booking clerk, and Mr.J. Gillard, ganger. It does give a reminder of just how many people were employed at what was not an overly busy location.

(Photos: Copyright Kidderminster Railway Museum)

Left: Netley station building in 1974. Comparing this with the photos of Woolston on page 144 the grander nature of the Netley building becomes apparent.

A Through Station

The line to Fareham opened on 2nd September 1889. It is likely that the turntable was removed at this time. However, the bulge in the boundary fence where it was can still be detected in 2011. For the opening of the new line the platforms were extended, and a footbridge provided. The LSWR minutes also record that the roofing for the footbridge was deferred, indefinitely as it turns out.

By the late 1890s the goods yard consisted of five sidings, all accessed from a trailing connection on the up line. Facing down the line were two sidings known as the up and hospital sidings. From these access could be made to the three up facing sidings known as the short road, middle (or crane) road, and the fence road.

A Junction

In 1900 the station became a junction with the opening of the hospital branch, which is detailed in the next section. Probably in

connection with the building of the branch, a short kickback siding appeared running from the fence road to a gravel pit. After this the next major development was doubling which took place between Netley and Woolston in May 1910, and to Swanwick in March 1911. At this time the goods yard was remodelled, with the kickback siding removed, and an extra down facing siding added.

Of course, during the First World War there was heavy traffic through Netley with ambulance trains running to and from the hospital, as well as additional traffic between Portsmouth and Southampton. As has been mentioned there were also extra trains in connection with the construction of Hamble airfield. During this time the stationmaster was Mr. G.W. Damen, who had been the first booking clerk at Swanage when that line opened in 1886. He was to remain in charge at Netley until his retirement in December 1926, by which time the station had come under the SR.

Right: BR Standard class 4 2-6-4 tank No.80084 shunts at Netley at an unknown date in the early 1960s. Meanwhile an identified *Hampshire* unit stands at the down platform with a Portsmouth-bound semi-fast. The goods shed is seen on the left.

(Photographer Unknown)

Left: In June 1963 *Hampshire* DEMU No.1117 is about to depart from Netley with a train for Southampton. Note the tail lamp still being carried, and the 'V'-shaped strip denoting that the guard's compartment was at this end of the train.
(Photo: John H.Bird Copyright SOUTHERN-images)

The Southern And World War Two

During the 1920s and 30s Netley settled to the life of a country station on a secondary line. However, there were busy days such as Whit Monday 1928, when the Hamble Air Pageant was held and 2,270 tickets were collected. Staff also took pride in the station. In 1937 the *Southern Railway Magazine* noted the array of window boxes and hanging baskets, as well as the flower garden on the down side.

The outbreak of war in 1939 again brought extra troop movements both on the hospital branch and the mainline. Although there does not seem to have been any air raid activity, the Luftwaffe seemingly respecting the medical facilities at the hospital. Later, it will seen how the station and branch contributed to the D-Day operations.

Nationalisation

Following the war and Nationalisation there was the usual pattern of gradual decline. The hospital branch effectively closed in 1955, although it was not formally taken out of use until December 1963, along with much of the goods yard, goods traffic having ceased on 22nd October 1962. In November 1964 the loading dock line was also abolished. *Hampshire* units had been introduced in 1957, but steam could still be seen on

through workings and goods trains.

In days past some of the through trains called at Netley, allowing the inhabitants direct access to places like Bristol and Cardiff. Today the station is served by a basic hourly electric service between Southampton and Portsmouth, supplemented in the peak. However, the station still has nearly 90,000 journeys starting or finishing there.

On the site of the former goods yard there is an industrial estate, but happily the station building has a grade 2 listing. The down waiting room and footbridge are also *in situ*. Even the signal box survives, but not at Netley. Closed in March 1980 when colour light signalling was introduced, it was salvaged for the Mid-Hants Railway and removed in May 1982. It is now in use at Ropley station. From Netley the line continues through Hamble, Bursledon and Swanwick to Fareham, but that is a story for another book.

Right: A party of schoolboys are off to a camp in this photo taken at Netley in July 1965.
(Photo: John H.Bird Copyright SOUTHERN-images)

Left: Netley signal box on 24th May 1962. Note that the box has been weather-boarded hiding the framing seen previously. This box has now been preserved at Ropley station on the Mid-Hants Railway.

(Photo: H.W.Robinson
Copyright J.F.Hyde, Steam Archive)

Right: The down waiting room at Netley in 1974. Comparison with the similar waiting room at Woolston on page 146 shows that these were part of the original structures built for the opening of the line in 1866. Originally it was open at the front, but was enclosed in 1895 at a cost of £20.

Left: An interesting manoeuvre at Netley in February 1966 as BR Standard class 4 No.75076 stands in the former goods yard with a parcels train. Meanwhile *Berkshire* unit No.1129 passes with an up train for Southampton.

(Photo: J.R.Fairman collection
Copyright Kidderminster Railway
Museum)

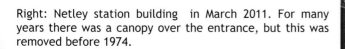

Right: Netley station building in March 2011. For many years there was a canopy over the entrance, but this was removed before 1974.

Netley Through the Years

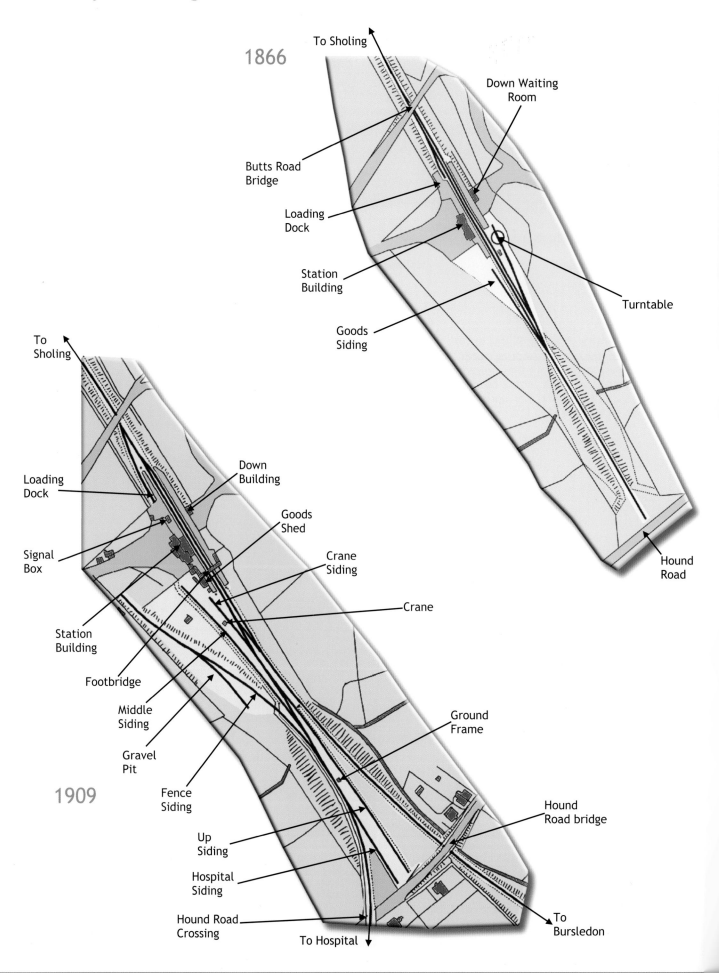

1866

To Sholing

Down Waiting Room

Butts Road Bridge

Loading Dock

Station Building

Goods Siding

Turntable

Hound Road

To Sholing

Loading Dock

Down Building

Goods Shed

Signal Box

Crane Siding

Crane

Station Building

Footbridge

Middle Siding

Gravel Pit

Ground Frame

Fence Siding

1909

Up Siding

Hospital Siding

Hound Road Crossing

To Hospital

Hound Road bridge

To Bursledon

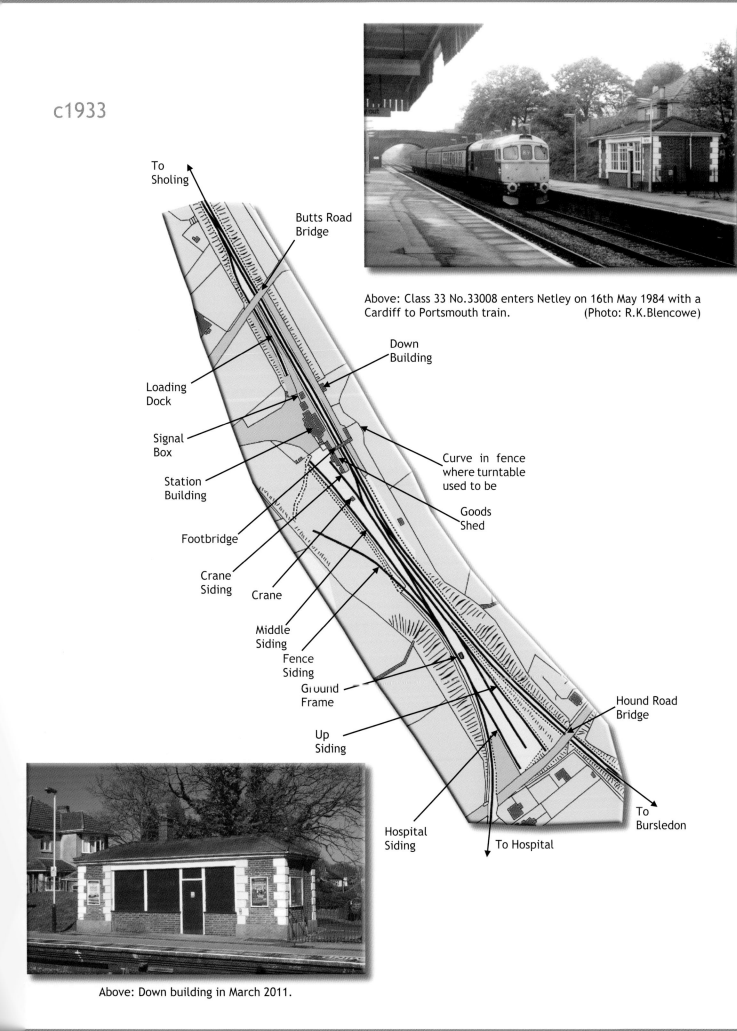

c1933

To Sholing

Butts Road Bridge

Above: Class 33 No.33008 enters Netley on 16th May 1984 with a Cardiff to Portsmouth train.   (Photo: R.K.Blencowe)

Down Building

Loading Dock

Signal Box

Station Building

Curve in fence where turntable used to be

Goods Shed

Footbridge

Crane Siding

Crane

Middle Siding

Fence Siding

Ground Frame

Up Siding

Hound Road Bridge

Hospital Siding

To Hospital

To Bursledon

Above: Down building in March 2011.

The Netley Hospital Branch

Left: A train, with '395' class 0-6-0 No.442 in charge, arrives at the Hospital station. The orderlies are lined up to help with the casualties.

(Photo: Lens of Sutton Association)

The Netley Hospital branch could well be said to have been built by Royal command. As has been seen, initially patients for Netley Hospital were dealt with at a platform adjoining the road to the hospital itself. However, the inadequacies of this arrangement soon became apparent, and the first request for a line directly into the hospital was made in 1872. Queen Victoria herself, also appears to have supported the idea in 1875, but nothing came of it.

In the early 1881 the wooden platform seems to have been replaced, and a shelter provided. Then in 1884 the LSWR obtained powers to build a line to the boundary of the War Department's land. This would have been 194 yards long on a 244 yard radius curve, but was not built at the time.

The three trips by Queen Victoria to the hospital in 1898 to visit those wounded on the North West Frontier, and in Africa, seem to have been the catalyst to the branch's construction. It is said the Queen took a particular interest in the project at the time. Certainly in 1898 the

hospital platform was extended, with a roof added, and a waiting room was provided in 1899. Finally, it was the outbreak of the second Boer War in 1899, that provided the impetus for the branch to be built.

In January 1900 authorisation was given for the construction of a 0.6 mile line costing £4,090. This had falling and rising gradients of 1 in 80 from the station to the hospital terminating with a 650ft long loop, with a 196ft platform. The loop was controlled from a ground frame which had its own building, and was unlocked with an Annett's key. There was also a carriage shed, capable of holding four ambulance carriages (otherwise known as ward cars), which could be heated from the hospital heating system. From the platform there was a covered way which gave direct access to the hospital.

The line received its first train on 18th April 1900, and less than a month later, on 16th May 1900, Queen Victoria came and made use of the line to visit over 500 troops, who had recently returned from South Africa. This was regarded as the official opening of the line. Therefore, in attendance that day were Col. Campbell, Chairman of the LSWR, Sam Fay, then the Traffic Superintendent and Dugald Drummond, the locomotive superintendent, as well as a crowd of hundreds.

Right: Possibly M7 No.106 was nearly new in this photograph of it taken at Netley Hospital station, as it was built in 1905 five years after the branch was opened. It also seems as if the driver is taking a nap! The carriage is one of the *Netley* cars.

(Photo: Lens of Sutton Association)

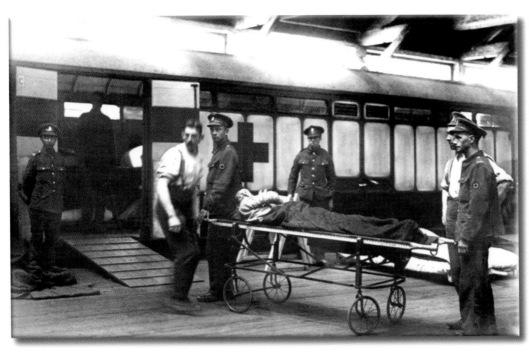

Left: Probably not taken at Netley but a photograph showing how the stretchers were loaded and unloaded from the ward cars.
(Photo: J.R.Fairman collection Copyright Kidderminster Railway Museum)

It is recorded that the Royal party departed Windsor just after 1pm arriving at the Hospital station at 3.52pm. From here Victoria was wheeled in her bath chair into the hospital to visit many of the troops, staying for an hour and half. It has to be said that at the age of eighty it was a remarkable effort, given her infirmities, but this was her last visit. However, it is worth recording that official Board of Trade approval for the line was not forthcoming until 21st May, although the inspection was carried out on 11th April 1900. One wonders what would have happened had there been an accident during Victoria's visit.

Of course during World War One the branch was well used with ambulance trains bringing in casualties from Southampton and elsewhere, and then trains going out to transfer patients to other facilities. It would not be until 20th June 1919 that it was recorded that the LSWR had not run any ambulance trains on its rails during the previous week. With the cessation of hostilities and coming under the Southern, services were less pressured.

World War Two

The gradients on the branch could prove a problem, and when three trains needed to depart from the hospital at the outbreak of World War Two with army medical personnel bound for embarkation at the docks this proved to be the case. Two trains with 'other ranks' and nurses successfully departed, but the third carrying the officers slipped on the grade and damaged the coupling rod to make the locomotive, a Drummond T9 4-4-0, totally immobile.

Interestingly during the war casualties

Right: Invalids arriving at Netley Hospital. These were obviously the walking wounded.
(Photo: Lens of Sutton Association)

were brought to Netley by road, and dispersed by train. It is recorded that no trains ran between Southampton docks and the hospital up until the end of 1943. Then a test train of 15 carriages with a locomotive at each end was run to the hospital from the docks on 23rd December 1943, probably as part of the preparations for D-Day. One train that did bring some interesting occupants to the branch ran in 1942, when a train arrived carrying horses from the cavalry regiment. The horses having been brought to graze in the grounds.

Meanwhile trains from Netley dispersed patients to a variety of destinations. These included Ardley, Stourport-on-Severn, Pangbourne, Mansfield, Bristol, Swindon, Chudleigh, Yeovil Junction, Moorhampton, Wymondham, Malvern Wells, Coalpit Heath, Barnwell, Tavistock and Ellesmere. In April 1944, in anticipation of what was to come, the branch was relaid in heavier rail, and on 9th June 1944 the first D-Day casualties arrived.

Nationalisation and Closure

After the war and railway Nationalisation, coupled with the rise in road transport, the branch was used less and less. The final train movement along it is recorded on 30th August 1955 when the last ward cars stored at the Hospital station were removed. In August 1960 the line

was rendered impassible due to a land-slip in Netley yard, but it was not until 1st December 1963 that it was formally taken out of use.

The hospital itself was demolished in 1967 except for the chapel and associated tower. Today much of the evidence of the branch has gone, although it is still possible to walk along part of the course of the line.

However, there is still steam at the Netley hospital site today. The area has been transformed into the Royal Victoria Country Park, and a group of volunteers built the 10¼ inch Royal Victoria Country Park Railway on the site, which first ran in 1996. This operates currently on a mile long loop of track, part of which runs alongside the trackbed of the former Hospital station.

Netley Hospital Branch in 1933

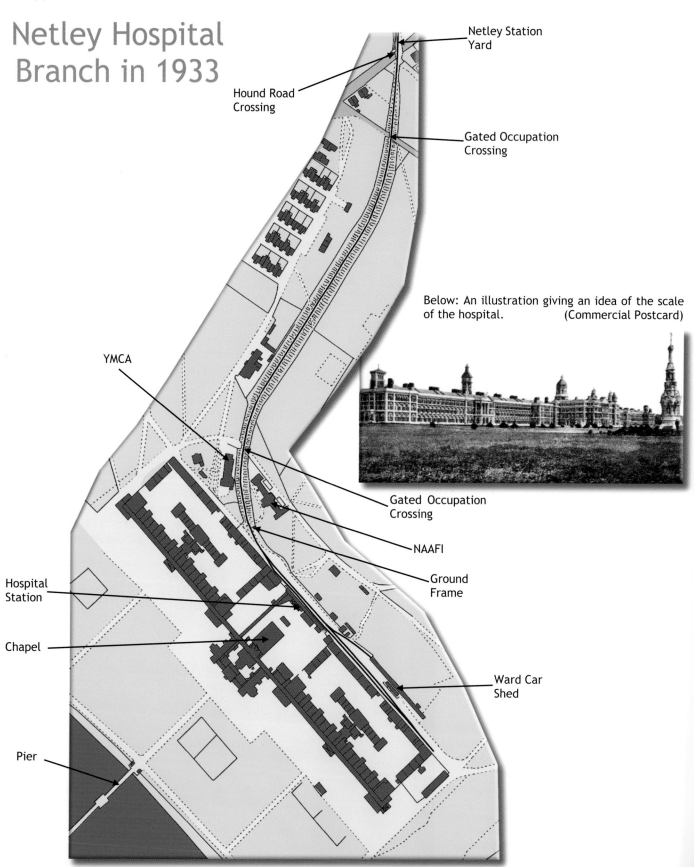

Below: An illustration giving an idea of the scale of the hospital. (Commercial Postcard)

Left: On 7th February 1955 BR Standard class 3 2-6-2 tank No.82012 stands in the ward car shed at Hospital station. This was connected to the hospital heating system so the ward cars could be heated in preparation for receiving patients, as well as having electrical connections for carriage lighting.
(Photo: J.R.Fairman collection Copyright Kidderminster Railway Museum)

Right: The site of the Hospital station in March 2011 looking along the line of the old trackbed. The building would have stretched to the far end of the car park. On the right is the former chapel, which is the only remaining part of the hospital.

Left: Looking towards the platform from the ward car shed siding on 7th February 1955. On the left are two ex-LSWR ward cars, the one on the right being W.D. No.1641 now undergoing restoration at the Pontypool and Blaenavon Railway.
(Photo: J.R.Fairman collection Copyright Kidderminster Railway Museum)

Right: The ground frame building at the Hospital station. The operating instructions for the branch in 1934 stated that it was worked by one engine in steam or by 'two or more engines coupled together' using the 'Pilot Guard' system. They would wear a red armband and have to accompany any train on the branch.

All facing points had to be padlocked or held by hand to permit the safe passage of trains. Before a train was permitted to leave the Hospital station the 'Pilot Guard' had to telephone the signalman at Netley to obtain permission to start. Also at least 15 minutes before any train traversed the line the stationmaster at Netley had to send someone to secure the gates on the three level crossings on the branch open, as well as arranging with the military authorities for the crossings to be manned.
(Photo: J.R.Fairman collection Copyright Kidderminster Railway Museum)

Left: Looking towards Netley station yard from the Ministry of Defence property in about 1952 we see two of the crossings referred to in the working instructions. The nearer crossing is an occupation crossing for an MOD road, and the far crossing is for Hound Road before the track enters the station yard.
(Photo: J.R.Fairman collection Copyright Kidderminster Railway Museum)

Right: Lifting the track on the hospital branch in October 1966, the remains of the hospital buildings can still be seen in the background.
(Photo: J.R.Fairman collection Copyright Kidderminster Railway Museum)

Left: The former trackbed in March 2011, looking towards Netley station.

Right: Steam can still be seen at the site of the Hospital station courtesy of the Royal Victoria Country Park Railway. Here the railway's 0-6-2 locomotive *Trevithick* is seen passing Chapel Road station in March 2011.

The Fawley Branch

Above: Towards the end of steam on Southern Region a number of excursions were run which included the Fawley branch in their itineraries. Here is one of these tours, promoted by the RCTS, departing from Marchwood towards Hythe with *USA* tanks Nos.30064 & 30073 in charge on 20th March 1966. (Photographer Unknown)

We have already seen that many of the early schemes for railway development along the Waterside were more concerned with developing alternative port facilities, particularly in connection with the Isle of Wight trade. However, it was the building of an oil refinery that led to the construction of a line between Totton and Fawley.

Conceived as the Totton, Hythe and Fawley Light Railway and originally promoted by the *Anglo Gulf West Indies Petroleum Co.* (AGWI) to serve their new refinery at Fawley, the railway was always going to be operated by the LSWR. The original course of the line was to be 9.12 miles from Totton to the refinery, passing through Marchwood and Hythe, at an estimated cost of £253,327. A Light Railway Order was applied for and a public inquiry held.

However, it was then decided that the LSWR would take over the company in July 1922. It resolved to make changes to the proposed route. One alteration was that the branch junction would be moved nearer to Totton by running the branch alongside the mainline. This meant that there was no need to have a separate signal box for the junction. The second variation was an eastward deviation at Hythe which brought the station nearer the centre of the town, and shortened its length.

Construction was placed in the hands of Robert McAlpine & Co Ltd at a cost of £117,276 in October 1923. Of course by now the SR had taken over the LSWR. Extensive use was made of concrete on the line for bridges, platforms

and buildings, so much so that it became known as *The Concrete Line*. The four overbridges were also designed for double track.

One of the features of the line, was the number of level crossings along its relatively short length. There were ten in total, only two of which initially had gates, as well as 32 occupation crossings.

Train Services

Originally when the line opened on 20th July 1925 there were five passenger trains in each direction daily, starting with a 6.52am from Eastleigh to Fawley. Trains for the rest of the day ran to Southampton Town, except one which terminated at Totton. However, these soon seem to have been reduced, and by 1926 no trains arrived at Fawley between early morning and late afternoon to suit the workers at the refinery. This was a pattern that would remain throughout the life of the line.

The lack of passengers on the line is also reflected in the fact that initially all the stations on the line fell under the jurisdiction of the stationmaster at Totton. Then in 1932 A.R.Wheeler was appointed stationmaster at Fawley, also responsible for Hythe and Marchwood.

Of course the line was mainly built to serve the refinery and the traffic that originated from it. Therefore, it is not surprising that goods traffic was significant, particularly petroleum products. Even the refinery had gone through

Left: A view from the early days of the Fawley branch of Adams O2 class No.191 arriving at Fawley. At this point No.191 still had a Drummond boiler, which was removed in May 1930, dating this shot to the 1925-30 period. The train is composed of six-wheeled carriages of the 1890s.

(Photo: Lens of Sutton Association)

changes. AGWI was bought by *British Mexican Petroleum*, otherwise branded as *Redline*. Then in 1925 it was in the hands of *Standard Oil*, at that time known as *Pratts*, but later by their familiar *Esso* brand from the 1930s.

Initially the main products carried by the railway were asphalt and bitumen contained in wooden barrels and loaded onto open wagons. There was also petrol and paraffin in tank wagons, these were to grow over the years along with gas oil, diesel, fuel oil and naphtha.

Southern Railway Magazine reported that on 31st July 1929 1,600 drums of petroleum pitch weighing 200 tons were dispatched from the site. An order was placed at 10am with the 31 wagons being delivered from the refinery at 8.45pm and departed at 10.15pm. In addition 19 tank wagons of petrol, three of asphalt, and three trucks of petroleum pitch plus other goods were dispatched from the station the same day. The following year on 23rd June it recorded that a special train of 45 wagons was run to clear the outward traffic from Fawley, and also a train consisting of 26 tank wagons, one batten truck and a van.

During the early days of the branch O2s were used to haul the passenger trains with A12 0-4-2 tender locomotives handling the goods traffic. Later in Southern days Q class

0-6-0s handled the freight turns, with Q1s being observed on the branch following their introduction in 1942.

The Second World War

In 1939 a siding was laid from Marchwood to Cracknore Hard, one and half miles distant. This was to eventually lead to the establishment of the Marchwood Military Port. Marchwood was also provided with the first crossing loop on the branch in 1943.

Despite the obvious target of the refinery in fact very little damage was suffered by the branch and refinery during the conflict. This was mainly because refining had ceased at Fawley for the duration, and it was simply used as a storage facility. Additional underground tanks were built, and new sidings laid.

Nationalisation

Following the war and Nationalisation the major development on the branch was the construction of a new refinery at Fawley. Building started in 1949 and the first phase was in production in 1951. By 1953 it was refining six million tons of oil annually. To serve the new refinery additional sidings were laid at Fawley.

		Week Days only										Week Days only			
Miles		mrn		aft	SO		aft	Miles			mrn	SX		SO	aft	aft
	London (Waterloo) K 324dep.	2ⓐ40	..		SX 1 30	..	3 30	3	Fawley (Hants)............dep	8 6	1150	..	1214	5 19	6 43
—	Southampton Terminus dep.		..	..	3 59	..	5 33	3	Hythe (Hants)................	8 14	1158	..	1222	5 27	6 51
1¼	Southampton Central... ıı	6 57	..	..	4 5	..	5 41	6	Marchwood	8 24	12 8	..	1232	5 38	7 1
2¼	Millbrook....................	7 2	..	..	4 8	..	5 47	9¾	Totton L 324	8 37	1220	..	1246	5 51	7 13
4¼	Redbridge....................	7 7	..	..	4 13	..	5 52	10¼	Redbridge 380	8 40	..	..	1248	5 54	7 16
5	Totton L...................	7 10	..	4 15	4 15	..	5 55	12	Millbrook	8 44	..	..	1253	5 59	7 20
8½	Marchwood.................	7 22	..	4 25	4 25	..	6 5	12¾	Southampton Cen. 330..arr.	8 48	..	..	1257	6 3	7 24
11½	Hythe (Hants)..............	7 32	..	4 35	4 35	..	6 15	14¼	Southampton G 494 .... ıı	9 2	..	..	..	..	7 31
14½	Fawley (Hants)........arr.	7 43	..	4 45	4 45	..	6 25	94	London (Waterloo) K 330 ..arr	11 0	..	..	4 16	8 37	1126

ⓐ Third class only   G Southampton Terminus (for Docks).   K Via Southampton Central.   L Station for Eling.
SO Saturdays only.   SX Saturdays excepted.
LOCAL TRAINS between Southampton and Redbridge, page 384—Southampton and Totton, page 324

The winter 1943 timetable for the Fawley branch.

Left: On 27th January 1951 a Z class 0-8-0 tank No.30950 is seen in charge of the morning freight for the branch between Central and Millbrook.
(Photo: P.M.Alexander Copyright Kidderminster Railway Museum)

In the 1950s further sidings were laid at Hardley, between Hythe and Fawley. The first served the *International Synthetic Rubber* depot and was laid in 1957, while the other was laid in 1959 to serve *Union Carbide Ltd.* Meanwhile, Hardley Halt had been opened nearby for the factory workers on 3rd March 1958.

New passing loops were laid on the branch in 1960. The first was at Marchwood where the old loop was extended across the level crossing, and was brought into use on 31st July 1960. Between Hythe and Fawley a new loop and signal box was provided just south of Frost Lane Crossing box, which opened on 16th October 1960. These allowed more flexible working to be introduced for freight trains, but no improved passenger service. By 1961 there were 25 train services on the line daily, the vast majority of which were freight workings.

During the 1950s and 60s the locomotives used on the branch changed. Under BR ex-LBSCR E4 and E5 classes were employed, along with T1s and M7s. In December 1950 Z class 0-8-0 tank locomotives appeared briefly, but were replaced by E6 0-6-2 tanks.

From 1952 ex-LMS and BR standard 2-6-2 tanks took over both freight and passenger workings. However, by 1960 increasing freight tonnage led to the introduction of H16 4-6-2 tank locomotives. These were joined in 1961 by members of the W class 2-6-4 tank locomotives, which later took over from the H16s.

From 1962 most passenger services were handled by *Hampshire* units, although some were still steam hauled. It was a *Hampshire* unit that comprised the last passenger service leaving at 4.53pm from Fawley on 11th February 1966.

Right: H16 class 4-6-2 tank locomotive No. 30517 is in charge of a train of tank wagons for the branch passing Cracknore Road footbridge between Central and Millbrook on 16th July 1960. Barrier wagons were added between the locomotives and the tank wagons to reduce the fire risk.
(Photographer Unknown)

Left: W class 2-6-4 tank No.31911 and an unidentified tank locomotive on a train from Fawley at Frost Lane crossing loop in April 1962.
(Photo: P.F.Bloxam)

Dieselisation

With the end of steam and passenger services, freight on the branch was in the hands of class 33 and 47 diesels for many years. In 1996 class 37s were seen on the branch. Later still class 58, 60 and 66 diesels have been used.

Meanwhile Fawley signal box closed in July 1978, and in November 1980 with new pipelines reducing the amount of oil being transported by rail, the Frost Lane loop was abolished. The Frost Lane signal box remained in use until 1st March 1981 after which the Marchwood box effectively controlled the whole branch.

Today traffic still flows along the branch, but at a reduced rate compared to the 1960s. A proposed development of new container berths near Marchwood and Dibden, which would have brought significant traffic to the branch has been turned down.

However, there have been constant suggestions of re-starting passenger services at least as far as Hythe on the branch, with the most recent study being instigated in 2009. But whether this will ever come to fruition remains to be seen, which leaves the future of the branch somewhat uncertain, with any significant shift in current traffic patterns from either Fawley or Marchwood bringing its viability into question.

Left: *Hampshire* unit No.1117 has arrived at Fawley on 27th July 1963 while an unidentified class 33, or *Cromptons* as they were known, is seen on the left.
(Photo: Norris Forrest Copyright transporttreasury.co.uk)

The Fawley Branch
Based on 1945 Ordnance Survey Map with Additions

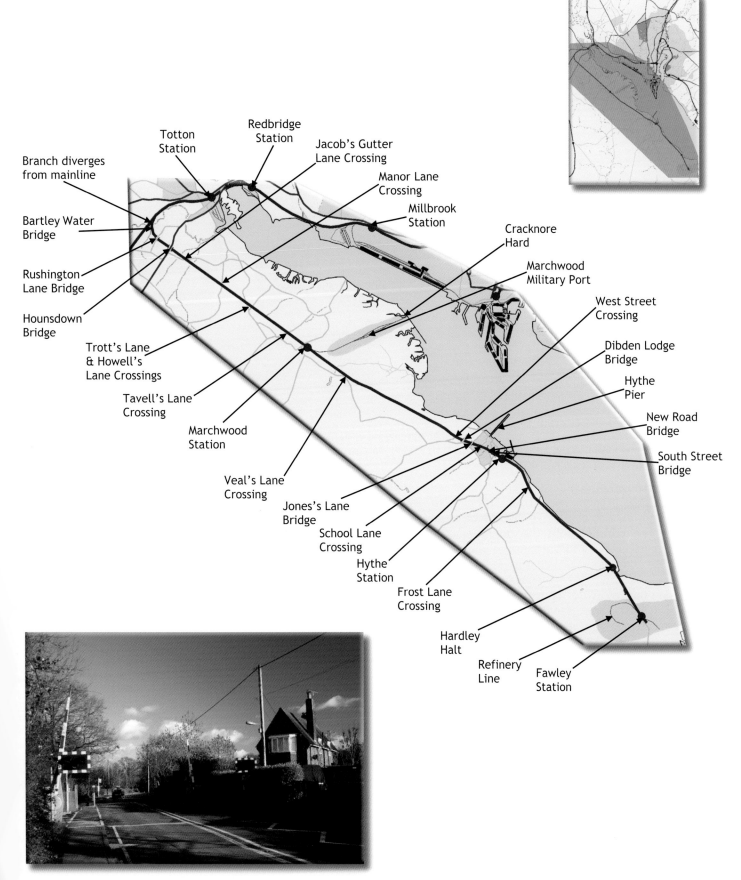

Branch diverges from mainline

Totton Station

Redbridge Station

Jacob's Gutter Lane Crossing

Manor Lane Crossing

Millbrook Station

Cracknore Hard

Bartley Water Bridge

Rushington Lane Bridge

Hounsdown Bridge

Marchwood Military Port

West Street Crossing

Trott's Lane & Howell's Lane Crossings

Dibden Lodge Bridge

Tavell's Lane Crossing

Hythe Pier

Marchwood Station

New Road Bridge

South Street Bridge

Veal's Lane Crossing

Jones's Lane Bridge

School Lane Crossing

Hythe Station

Frost Lane Crossing

Hardley Halt

Refinery Line

Fawley Station

Above: Jacob's Gutter Lane crossing in January 2011.

Marchwood

Above: *USA* class tanks Nos.30069 and 30064 stand at Marchwood with the LCGB *Hampshire Branch Lines Railtour* on 9th April 1967. Note the cement silo in the goods yard at this time. From Marchwood the train travelled to Fawley before returning to Totton where it featured in the photo on page 130. (Photo: Copyright Colour-Rail342248)

At Totton no additional passenger facilities were provided for the new branch, most trains running to and from Southampton. For about five-eighths of a mile the new branch ran parallel with the Bournemouth down line before curving away to the south, climbing on a grade of 1 in 100.

Crossing Bartley Water on a three arch concrete bridge, the branch then passes under Rushington Lane bridge and into a cutting. The next landmarks are the Hounsdown overbridges, the original one of which carried the A35 across the line. When a new dual carriageway was built parallel to the old road, a second bridge was constructed alongside to the first on the north side to carry the new road.

The next section to Jacob's Gutter Lane crossing has become quite built up in recent years. Crossing gates were not provided here until March 1937, in part due to an accident that happened on 26th July 1933. Then the 4.05pm train from Fawley headed by A12 class locomotive No.641 was in collision with a 30 cwt Chevrolet lorry. The lorry driver was killed and his mate seriously injured.

Interestingly the coroner's inquest put the blame on the locomotive driver for driving negligently. However, the Railway Inspector disagreed, and said the lorry driver was

at fault, but he recommended the erection of gates at the crossing. But, despite a 1934 census which showed that 636 vehicles used the crossing daily, these did not materialise, until at least one more collision happened there. A crossing keeper's house was provided when the gates were installed, and in August 1966 the gates were replaced by lifting barriers.

Moving south the branch crosses the A326, otherwise known as the Marchwood by-pass, on an overbridge erected in 1960. Running now with Bull's Copse on the right the line comes to the next crossing at Manor Lane, which today is an occupation crossing. Then a little further on there is Trott's Lane crossing, that was provided with barriers in 1966. Passing through the woods the next crossing at Howell's Lane, now closed, came quickly. Remember that all these crossings were originally unguarded with a 10 mph speed limit, and the locomotive driver had to sound his whistle on the approach to each one.

Pooksgreen now lies to the right, with a series of gravel pits on the left, and the line crosses Tavell's Lane, again provided with barriers in 1966. The line today runs through the outskirts of Marchwood before it encounters what was the first, of the two originally, gated crossings on the branch, at Main Road. Beyond the crossing lies

Left: What appears to be a 'W' class 2-6-4 tank passes through Marchwood with a mixed freight in the early 1960s.
(Photographer Unknown)

Marchwood station, three and a half miles from Totton.

Here the station originally consisted of a single platform 350ft long and 12ft wide, with a single storey station building built of concrete blocks covered with pebbledash. The crossing gates were manually operated, and still are today, while the signals were controlled from a frame in the booking office. Beyond the station was a goods loop, with two sidings which were laid behind the platform.

From the loop in 1939 a siding was laid to Cracknore Hard, later to become Marchwood Military Port. In November 1943 the original frame in the booking office was replaced with a second-hand seventeen-lever frame, and an extension was made to the building to serve as a signal box. It is also possible that the shorter of the two sidings was removed at this time.

Originally the line was worked by Tyer's No. 6 Electric Tablet as a single section from Eling Jct to Fawley. But with the new arrangements at Marchwood the line was split into two sections, Eling to Marchwood, operated by Tyer's Electric Key Token, and Marchwood to Fawley by Tyer's No.7 Tablets. The latter was replaced by Electric Key Tokens in 1959.

Later in 1960 the passing loop was extended past the platform and across the level crossing. Both roads are signalled for bi-directional running and sand drags were added at each end.

Marchwood of course lost its passenger service in February 1966, but goods traffic continued to flow both to Fawley and the Military Port. In June 1971 the remaining siding was taken out of use, and lifted. Then on February 28th 1982 the token system was replaced with the Track Circuit Block system. However, the Marchwood box still retains control of the branch with information being shared with Eastleigh box.

Today Marchwood station still has a signalman on duty, and trains move through to and from Fawley as well as to the Port, although not to the extent that they used to. Of course if a passenger service was restored to the line then the station could take on a whole new life, and help ease traffic flows into Southampton.

Right: An unidentified class 73 stands at Marchwood having emerged from the Military port with a mixed freight in 1978.

Above: Class 2 2-6-2 tank No.41305 and W class No.31916 near Pooksgreen north of Marchwood on 28th July 1961.
(Photo: R.Amos Copyright Kidderminster Railway Museum)

Above: Class 66 No.66049 running light crosses Marchwood level crossing, still with manually operated gates in August 2001.

Left: The exterior of Marchwood station building in 1978. This view is now impossible to get because of the development that has taken place around the station.

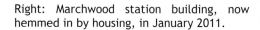

Right: Marchwood station building, now hemmed in by housing, in January 2011.

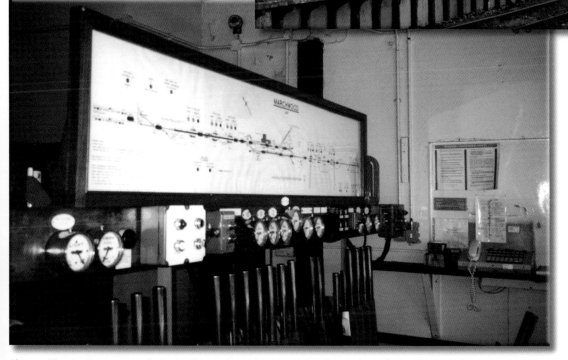

Above: The indicator panel at Marchwood station in August 2001; from here the signalman controls the whole branch.

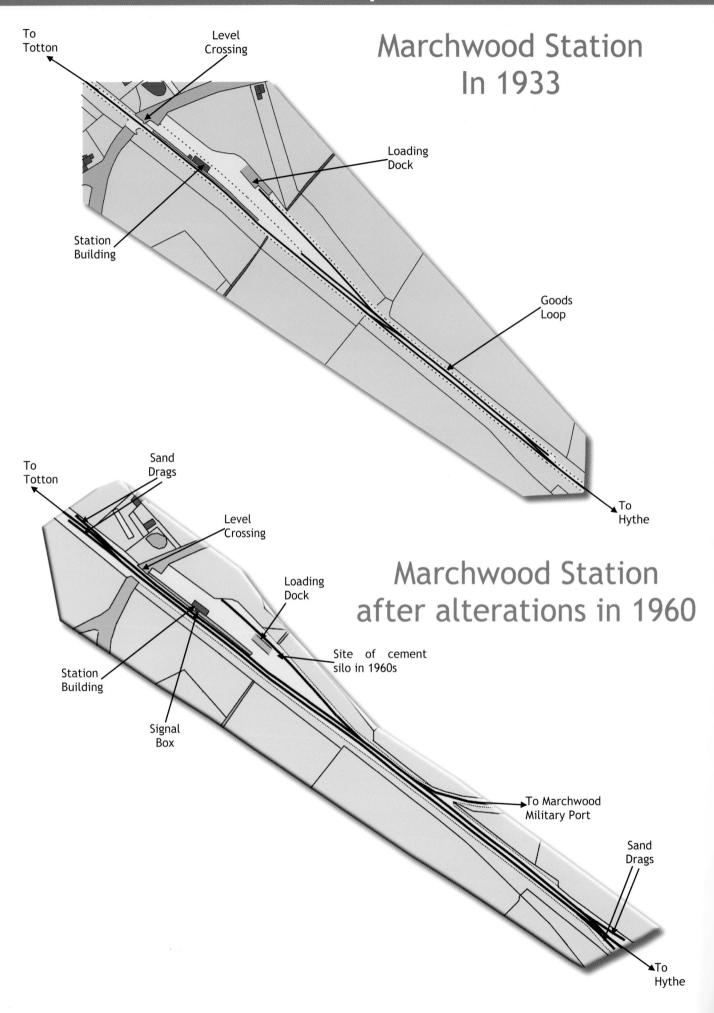

Marchwood Station
In 1933

To
Totton

Level
Crossing

Loading
Dock

Station
Building

Goods
Loop

To
Hythe

Marchwood Station
after alterations in 1960

To
Totton

Sand
Drags

Level
Crossing

Loading
Dock

Site of cement
silo in 1960s

Station
Building

Signal
Box

To Marchwood
Military Port

Sand
Drags

To
Hythe

Marchwood Military Port

Above: For several months in 1978 the author worked at the Central Electricity Generating Board's Marchwood Engineering Labs, based next door to the Military Port, and was able to witness some of the activities on the Military Railway during his lunch-breaks. However on 22nd July 1978 they held an open day which gave an opportunity to look round the facility. Here the then only remaining steam locomotive, *Waggoner*, and the railway's entire passenger stock is seen in action.

I am very grateful to Major Ross Mason of the Marchwood Military History Cell on whose notes the information in this section is based. He writes:

Sometimes some pretty big road vehicles and trailers come in and out of the Sea Mounting Centre (previously known as Marchwood Military Port), and it is always wise to give them the right of the road. But they are not top dogs there, as there is a sign just inside the port gate with the notice 'Beware of and Give Way to Trains' so far, for many years, they have.

Who are these Kings of the military castle then? Enter the Marchwood Military Railway (MMR). It may not be the oldest military railway still running, but it is the only one with a recognised timetable for many decades.

The story of the railway began in World War Two on 28th

November 1943 when the MMR came into operation. This was when Marchwood Military Port was being constructed on reclaimed land by the Royal Engineers. Originally there were 22 miles of track. Some of this was used to fabricate, using rail wagons, the 'Beetle' and 'Whale' components of the Mulberry Harbours.

These were gradually moved towards the waterfront for launching into Southampton Water, prior to movement to Normandy. A feature of the rail system was the traverser to move components sideways as required for a particular track at the waterfront. The concrete base of this still exists today. Other parts of the track were used for the reception and turn-round of mainline locomotives and for serving stores depots. Originally all locomotives were steam, including a steam crane and were operated by Royal Engineers soldiers.

Right: Following the end of the Second World War considerable rationalisation of the track at the Port took place. However, the north side became the location for the building of Marchwood power station. During its construction a connection was made to the MMR in 1955 to enable materials to be transferred to the site.
Here on 22nd January 1956 WD 157 *Constantine*, a Hunslet Austerity built in 1945, is seen at the gates to the power station site on the other side of Cracknore Lane from the Port. Materials were handled on the construction site by the CEGB's own locomotives. Tracks remained around the power station until 1963.
(Photo: D.Cull Copyright Kidderminster Railway Museum)

Left: A further view by the author of *Waggoner* and its train on 22nd July 1978. The carriages were still used for the daily shuttle services between the living quarters and jetty.

Some half a dozen steam locomotives are known to have served at Marchwood (For more details see Dave Marden's *A Further Look at Southampton's Quayside Railways*), but *Waggoner* was to be the last, being transferred to the Museum of Army Transport at Beverley in June 1984. However, we were destined to meet again, as will be seen on page 179.

After the war the port was retained and 17 Port Training Regiment RE was formed and four Port Regiments of the Army Emergency Reserve were based on the now forgotten names of Roberts and Highlands camps. Gradually civilians took over the operational rail duties and over the years have been responsible to numerous different headquarters, but the name did not change. It is now part of the Joint Supply Chain Rail and Container Service.

The choice of Marchwood for a military port was influenced by the good communications to the hinterland. These included access to the Southampton to Fawley branch line. Access to the port is made just south of Marchwood station leading to a set of reception sidings. Here the mainline locomotive is taken off, either to take out a train or to go light to the Southampton area. Originally one track led to the jetty, with intermediate sidings along the way, some leading to workshops and store sheds.

In the late 1980s the railway was extensively refurbished when the Military Port was modernised, which included the construction of a new jetty. This was served by rail with a set of regulating sidings being laid to it. A connection between the old and new jetty lines was put in to ease cross jetty operation.

A feature of the railway has been the expertise and loyalty of the civilian staff, who have had to meet sudden emergencies, usually on a Friday afternoon. For instance the build-up for the Falkland Islands campaign was a period of intense activity. So was that for the first Gulf War, which occupied the MMR for over a year. Subsequent operations in the Balkans, Iraq, and Afghanistan have all involved the MMR, which has always coped with sudden increases in traffic. It is always ready for the unexpected.

Major Ross Mason

Left: Mainline trains entered the site from the Fawley branch at Marchwood station, and the mainline locomotive would be detached. Sometimes it would return light engine, or it would be used to haul another train from the Port. Here in 1978 an unidentified Class 73 Electro-Diesel waits to move onto the branch. The walkway gave access to Mulberry Halt, which was at the start of the daily passenger shuttle.

Photographs of the port are of course limited, I am therefore very grateful to Winston McCanna for supplying these views. At the time these were taken he was Railway Supt. at Marchwood, and later Chief Mechanical Engineer for Army Railways.

Left: A close-up view of Ruston & Hornsby 0-6-0 diesel shunter No.432 built in 1962 with class 47 No. 47257 in the early 1980s. No.432 was based at Marchwood between 1974 and 1986, being scrapped in 2004.

(Photo: W.McCanna)

Right: A general view from the exchange sidings at Marchwood looking towards the jetties. No.47257 is departing with its train, with No.432 on its left. On the right is the substantially equipped loco shed which was rebuilt c1973.

(Photo: W.McCanna)

Below: No.432 and No.425, being prepared to welcome home the troops from the Falklands. No.425 was a Ruston and Hornsby 0-6-0 built in 1961. It was based at Marchwood between 1973 and 1986.

(Photo: W.McCanna)

Left: Marchwood continued to operate a daily passenger service long after such services ceased on other lines. Here is the daily train with No.432 in charge. However, because the brake end coach was being repainted BR had lent an ex-SR 25-ton bogie brake van to substitute.
(Photo: W.McCanna)

Right and below: The Falklands campaign had provided a major logistical challenge to the staff at Marchwood. However, there was some cause for celebration in July 1982 when the troops, and two of the Marchwood-based ships returned. However, this was a bitter-sweet moment for one of the ships sent out, *Sir Galahad*, never returned, and another was severely damaged. Those who gave their lives would not be forgotten.
(Photos: W.McCanna)

Plan of Marchwood Military Port in the 1950s

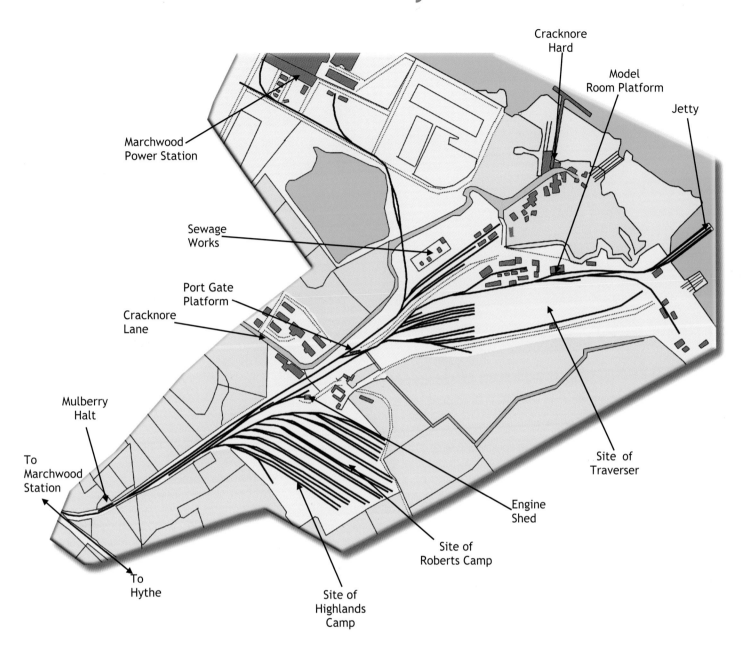

Cracknore Hard

Model Room Platform

Jetty

Marchwood Power Station

Sewage Works

Port Gate Platform

Cracknore Lane

Mulberry Halt

To Marchwood Station

To Hythe

Site of Highlands Camp

Site of Roberts Camp

Engine Shed

Site of Traverser

Left: Sometimes interesting things happen in life. In 2005, after the closure of the Museum of Army Transport at Beverley, *Waggoner* was transferred to the Isle of Wight Steam Railway. Here it is at Havenstreet station on 11th November 2009 having hauled the launch train for the first volume of *Southern Rails on the Isle of Wight*.

Hythe

Above: *Berkshire* unit No.1131 with No.1128 coupled to the rear approaches Hythe from Fawley with the *Fawley Flyer* railtour on 23rd April 1978.
(Photo: R.Newman)

From Marchwood towards Hythe the train passed over the occupation crossing for Pumpfield Farm. Now the train passes Post Copse on the left and passes over Veal's Lane crossing, which was also provided with barriers in 1966, and into Long Copse. Emerging from the copse, the track now crosses open fields with the estuary of the River Test on the left, and passes over an occupation bridge.

West Street crossing is then reached on the outskirts of Hythe. Here in the 1950s & 60s there was a sad tale of 'buck-passing', which contributed to the death of a passenger in a Volkswagen car. This was in collision with the 8.06am train from Fawley to Southampton on 15th September 1961.

In 1958 half-barriers were recommended for both Frost Lane and West Street, the latter to be provided at a cost of £5,067. The Inspector at the time recommended that the railway and Hampshire County Council shared the costs, and the railway thought the Council had agreed. However, later the Council refused to pay denying they had any responsibility, and there was deadlock. In November 1960 the Council asked the Minister of Transport to order the railway to install the barriers, but still this was not done.

Following the accident, which the Inspector said was the responsibility of the car driver, it was recommended that the Council should pay a contribution towards the barriers. These were eventually installed in June 1962. Interestingly it was stated at the enquiry that there was only one passenger on the train, who was a railway clerk,

testifying to the limited passenger numbers on the line.

Now in a cutting the line passes under the Dibden Lodge overbridge, and then under Jones's Lane bridge. Next came the gated crossing at School Lane, where a crossing keeper's house was provided. Barriers have never been fitted here and the gates are still manually operated.

The track is now on an embankment and runs behind Hythe town centre, passing over New Road and then South Street underbridges. After these, Hythe station is reached three miles from Marchwood.

Like Marchwood, Hythe station was a simple affair with a single platform, pebble-dashed station building, slightly smaller than Marchwood, water column and water tank. Being on such a high embankment substantial concrete foundations had to be sunk to level the site. Passenger services ceased with the rest of the branch.

At the station there was also a single siding and loading dock. However below the station on the north side of the line there was a further goods yard. This was accessed from a trailing connection near Frost Lane crossing almost half a mile distant. Two sidings were provided on the site which adjoined the *Supermarine* Aviation Works. The siding at the station was decommissioned in September 1969, and the lower sidings taken out of use in December 1970. Today the former goods yard is a housing estate, and the station building still exists as the Waterside Heritage Centre. It would be the terminus of any proposed restoration of passenger services.

Left: North of Hythe there are two overbridges. On 26th April 1962 BR class 2 2-6-2 tank No.41319 passes under the second of these at Jones's Lane with a train for Fawley. The first vehicle in the train appears to be a Syphon 'G', some of which were built by BR in the 1950s to a GWR design.
(Photo: Colin Hogg/Courtesy Bluebell Railway Museum Archive)

Right: Supposedly the first passenger train to arrive at Hythe from Fawley on 25th July 1925. However, there seems little sign of celebratory decorations, and the crowds seem somewhat sparse.
(Photo: Lens of Sutton Association)

Left: M7 0-4-4 tank No.30378 is seen on the 12.14pm from Fawley to Southampton at Hythe on 23rd December 1950. On the left can be seen the *Supermarine* works in front of which was the lower goods yard.
(Photo: K.G.Carr Copyright P.Fidczuk)

Left: BR class 2 tank No.41305 at Hythe with a train for Fawley on 23rd April 1960. Apparently rose trees were being loaded into the luggage compartment.
(Photo: J.Harrold Copyright transporttreasury.co.uk)

Right: M7 0-4-4 tank No.30032 is seen at Hythe with a train for Fawley on 11th June 1959. By this time the water column which stood more or less opposite the station building has disappeared.
(Photo:A.E.Bennett Copyright transporttreasury.co.uk)

Left: Just three months later, on 22nd September 1959, Jim Aston also photographed Hythe station. However, the eagle-eyed will notice that by this time the water tower has also been demolished.
(Photo J.H.Aston)

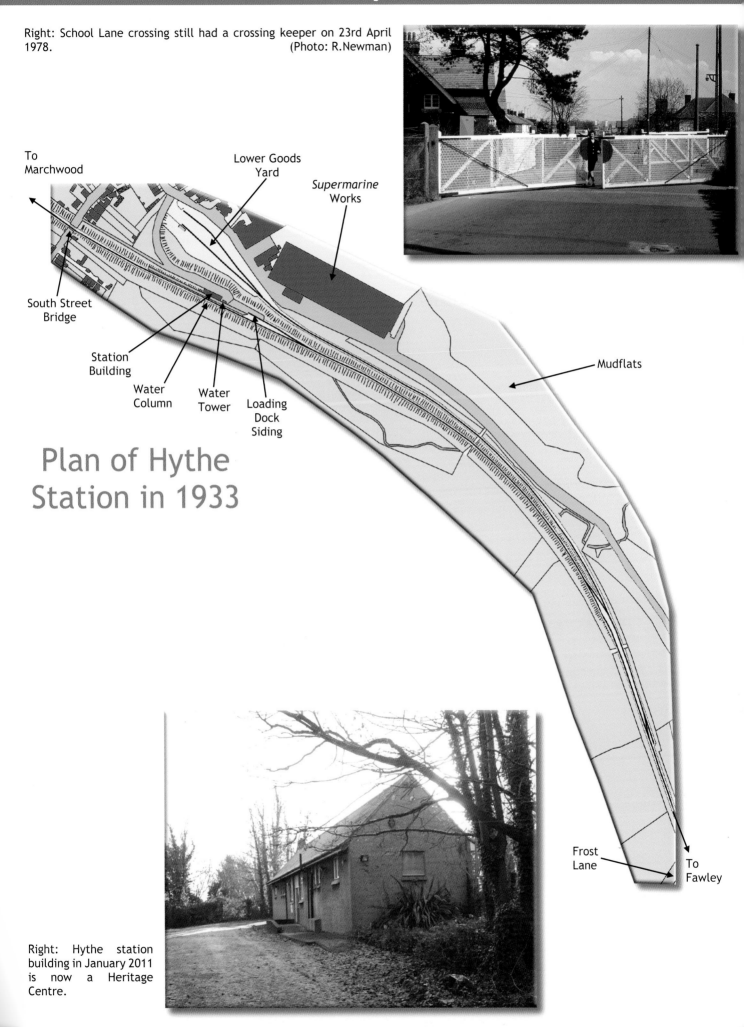

Right: School Lane crossing still had a crossing keeper on 23rd April 1978.
(Photo: R.Newman)

To Marchwood

Lower Goods Yard

Supermarine Works

South Street Bridge

Station Building

Water Column

Water Tower

Loading Dock Siding

Mudflats

Plan of Hythe Station in 1933

Frost Lane

To Fawley

Right: Hythe station building in January 2011 is now a Heritage Centre.

Frost Lane Crossing

Left: Circa 1958 M7 No.30033 0-4-4 tank is seen at Frost Lane crossing with a train for Fawley. Note that the crossing is completely open at this time, and typical of most of the crossings on the line up until the 1960s. The photographer is standing on the site of what would be Frost Lane Crossing signal box.

(Photo: M. Roberts Copyright Kidderminster Railway Museum)

Right: Frost Lane Crossing box was opened on 16th October 1960, but the crossing remained open until 1963 when barriers were installed. It is seen here on 27th August 1968.

(Photo: K.G.Carr Copyright P.Fidczuk)

Left: On 27th August 1968 the signalman on duty makes use of the token platform to exchange tokens with the driver of a class 33 with an oil train. The crossing loop was on the side of the road where the photographer was standing.

(Photo: K.G.Carr Copyright P.Fidczuk)

Right: Frost Lane Crossing loop was abolished in November 1980 only twenty years after it was opened, and the signal box closed the following March. In January 2011 there were hardly any traces of the box left.

Fawley

Above: 2-6-2 tank locomotive No.41328 built by BR in 1952 waits to depart from Fawley on an unknown date with coach set 823.
(Photo: Copyright Colour-Rail 304457)

Now the train leaves Hythe for the final three miles to Fawley. Just out from the station the line passes over an occupation bridge for a footpath to Langdown Park. Since passing under the A35 at Hounsdown the branch has been running in near-enough a straight line in a south easterly direction. Now the track curves south coming close to the shoreline, and descending on a grade of 1 in 264 to Frost Lane crossing, three-quarters of a mile from Hythe station.

It was here that one of the earliest accidents on the line occurred when on 15th November 1926 a special goods train of eight empty wagons, being hauled by A12 class 0-4-2 No.605, was in collision with a car. The Inspector again blamed the car driver but stated that the visibility of the crossing should be improved.

As has been seen earlier, in 1958 it was recommended that barriers be fitted here. However, this was delayed with the scheme to build a loop and signal box at the crossing. These were commissioned on 16th October 1960, but barriers were not provided on the crossing until 30th June 1963, and even then they were mechanically operated.

The loop only lasted until 30th November 1980, with the box being retained simply to operate the barriers. However, in March 1981 automatic barriers were fitted to the crossing and the box was closed. Today, no trace of the loop or box remain.

From Frost Lane the rails curve south east again along the shoreline. Originally the line passed through Newlands Copse and Great Styles Wood, but later this area was industrialised. The first factory to be encountered was the *Union Carbide* plant on the up side of the line. This was served by a single trailing siding operated by a ground frame from May 1959. Next comes the site of Hardley Halt, opened in March 1958 and closed in April 1965, again on the up side of the line. It never appeared in any public timetable simply consisting of a single concrete platform for the workers.

Behind the halt was the *International Synthetic Rubber Co.* which was served by two sidings from a trailing connection. These sidings came into use in June 1957, and remain *in situ*. From here trains pass through Lammas Wood and approach Cadland Quay, where there was an occupation crossing, but now on the west of the line a reservoir has been created with the track bridging the outflow.

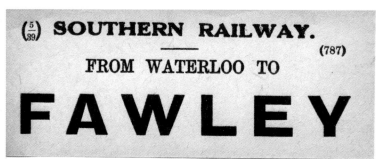

Left: Hardley Halt was a basic structure as seen here, although it did have lighting.
(Photo: Lens of Sutton Association)

After this the line enters the main refinery site. To the west are the extensive Cadland sidings which came into use in April 1950. From these a line runs north curving round through nearly 270 degrees into the new refinery. This was originally used to handle construction traffic, but still remains *in situ*.

Back on the main branch, opposite Cadland sidings on the down side of the line is a double loop built for the loading of Liquid Petroleum Gas. This came into use on 26th August 1960. Also on the down side of the line there were originally two parallel loop lines for goods trains. Later in 1952 another loop was laid on the up side, presumably in connection with the Cadland sidings.

The 'mainline' now passes over an occupation crossing created in 1950 to permit access to the facilities on the east side of the tracks. After this comes the site of the original goods yard on the up side, which had a goods shed moved to the site from Tisted by the SR in 1927. Originally only two sidings were provided, but this was later extended with a new series of four sidings laid out to the west to serve the underground storage tanks built in 1940. Of these the two original sidings remain, but two of the wartime sidings have been removed.

Trains enter the station platform three miles from Hythe, and it seems strange that an 'ordinary' terminus existed in the middle of this industrial complex. Here was a signal box built to the standard LSWR design of the turn of the twentieth century. There was also a station building to the same design as Marchwood, a run round loop, and a water tower added possibly when the platform was extended in 1951. All the buildings along with the goods shed have now been demolished. The signal box was closed on 9th July 1978.

Opposite the station is the line, through the boundary gate, to the AGWI sidings, one of which curves away towards the jetties, while to the south east there are further loading facilities for tank wagons. Within the complex the refinery operates its own locomotives. Today there is no public access to the station, surrounded as it is by the refinery plant. Therefore, it is unlikely that any restored passenger service would operate this far. However, hopefully the oil traffic will continue to flow for many years.

Right: Again supposedly the first train to arrive at Fawley, but once more there is too little sign of celebrations or the civic welcome, mentioned in descriptions of the event, for this to be likely.
(Photo: Lens of Sutton Association)

Left: Fawley station seen from the north on 23rd December 1950. The additional weather protection on the awning for the goods shed is worth noting. The water tower was added in front of the hut on the left.

(Photo: K.G.Carr Copyright P.Fidczuk)

Right: M7 No.30379 arrives with the 4.06pm from Southampton Central on 22nd September 1959 across the occupation crossing just before the station. Tank wagons can be seen in Cadland sidings in the background. The nearest turnout in the left foreground is part of the original station goods yard, while the point behind leads to the sidings built in conjunction with the underground storage tanks during World War Two.

(Photo: J.H.Aston)

Left: Two BR standard class 3 2-6-2 tanks, Nos. 82014 and 82016, stand by the water tower, which was ex-GWR from Warminster, at Fawley on 13th May 1960.

(Photo: J.H.Aston)

Left: Fawley signal box on 23rd April 1978. Behind the box is one of the underground storage tanks built during World War Two.
(Photo: R.Newman)

Right: The *Fawley Flyer* special at Fawley on the same occasion. *Berkshire* unit No.1131 stands by the station building. An indication of how the station is dwarfed by its setting is given by the storage tank behind.

(Photo: R.Newman)

Left: In what was probably the last weeks that Fawley box was open, the token is exchanged with the driver of a class 33 and oil train arriving at the station. Fawley box closed on 9th July 1978.

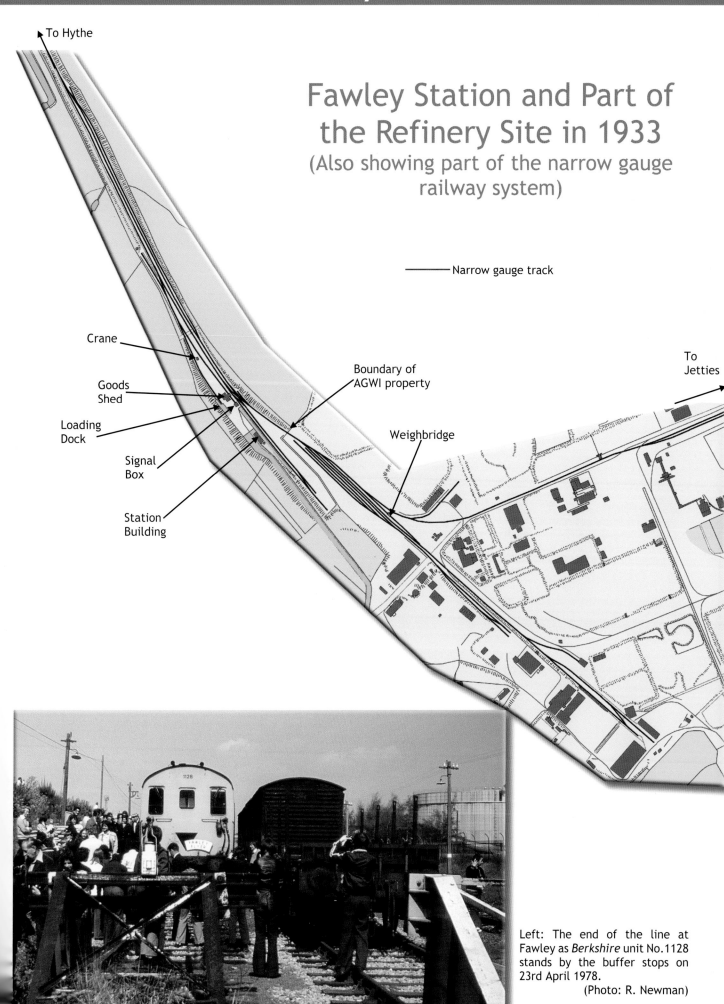

To Hythe

Fawley Station and Part of the Refinery Site in 1933
(Also showing part of the narrow gauge railway system)

———— Narrow gauge track

Crane

Goods Shed

Loading Dock

Signal Box

Station Building

Boundary of AGWI property

Weighbridge

To Jetties

Left: The end of the line at Fawley as *Berkshire* unit No.1128 stands by the buffer stops on 23rd April 1978.

(Photo: R. Newman)

And Finally

Above: We end with another iconic shot of the old Southampton Central as *Merchant Navy* No.35002 *Union Castle* takes water at the head of the up *Pines Express* on 27th July 1963. In less than a year the locomotive would be withdrawn, and only a couple of years after that the clock tower would be no more. (Photo: N.Nicholson Copyright transporttreasury.co.uk)

Bibliography

A Further Look at Southampton's Quayside Railways, D.Marden, Kestrel Railway Books, 2009

British Railways Operating History Southern Region Part 3 Wessex, T.S.Bradshaw, Xpress Publishing

Castleman's Corkscrew Vol.1 The Nineteenth Century, B.L.Jackson, Oakwood Press, 2007

Castleman's Corkscrew Vol.2 The Twentieth Century and Beyond, B.L.Jackson, Oakwood Press, 2008

Chapel Crossing, M. Snellgrove, *Track Topics*, Southern Counties Railway Society, March and April 1975

Farewell to the Floating Bridges, J.Horne, Southampton City Transport and the Southampton University Industrial Archaeology Group, 1976

Gradients of the British Main-Line Railways, The Railway Publishing Co. Ltd., 1947

History of the Southern Railway, C.F.Dendy Marshall Revised R.W.Kidner, Ian Allan, 1963 & 1982

Locomotives of the London and South Western Railway, Vols.1&2, D.L.Bradley, Railway Correspondence and Travel Society, 1965, 1967

LSWR Carriages Volume One, G.R.Weddell, Wild Swan Publications, 1992

Making Tracks, J.R.Fairman, Kingfisher Railway Productions, 1988

Netley Hospital and Its Railways, J.R.Fairman, Kingfisher Railway Productions, 1984

Off the Rails, B.Bishop, Kingfisher Railway Productions, 1984

Refugees in an Age of Genocide: Global, National and Local Perspectives during the Twentieth Century, K.Knox & T.Kushner, Routledge, 1999

Signal Box Diagrams of the Great Western and Southern Railways Vol. 9, G.A.Pryer

South Coast Railways - Portsmouth to Southampton, V.Mitchell & K.Smith, Middleton Press, 1986

South Coast Railways - Southampton to Bournemouth, V.Mitchell & K.Smith, Middleton Press, 1987

Southampton's Quayside Steam, D.Marden, Kestrel Railway Books, 2007

Southampton's Railways, B.Moody, Atlantic Publishers, 1992, 1997

Southern Electric 1909-1979, G.T.Moody, Ian Allan, 1957 & 79

Southern Main Lines Woking to Southampton, V.Mitchell & K.Smith, Middleton Press, 1988

Southern Rails on the Isle of Wight Vol.1, I.Drummond, Holne Publishing, 2009

The Fawley Branch, J.R.Fairman, Oakwood Press, 2002

The History of the Southern Railway, M.R.Bonavia, Unwin Hyman, 1987

The London and South Western Railway Vol.1, R.A.Williams, David & Charles, 1968

The London and South Western Railway Vol.2, R.A.Williams, David & Charles, 1973

The London and Southampton Railway Companion, A.Freeling, J.T.Norris, 1839

The LSWR in the Twentieth Century, J.N.Faulkner & R.A.Williams, David & Charles, 1988

The Midland and South Western Junction Railway, C.G.Maggs, David & Charles, 1967, 1980

The Southampton and Netley Railway, E.Course, Southampton Record Office, 1973

The Waterloo-Southampton Line, R.W.Kidner, Oakwood Press, 1983

To The Railway Born, T.Carter, Silver Link Publishing Ltd, 1992

Transport History Vol.2 No.3, *Southampton and the Railway Mania*, D.J.Rowe, David & Charles, 1969

War on the Line, B.Darwin, Middleton Press, 1946, 1984, 1993, 1998

Plus various editions of **Backtrack**, **British Railways Magazine**, **Southern Railway Magazine**, and **The Railway Magazine**.

Primary resources consulted include:
British Library Newspaper Archive
LSWR Minute Books
Various records at the Hampshire Record Office, National Archives at Kew, Southampton Record Office

Web-Resources consulted include:
Southern E-group pages at www.semgonline.com
The railtour files at www.sixbellsjunction.co.uk
Wikipedia at www.wikipedia.com
Station usage statistics from Office of Rail Regulation at www.rail-reg.gov.uk

Coming Soon

Southern Rails On Southampton Docks

Including:

The Development of the Railways of Southampton Docks
Boat Trains
Building of the New Docks
The Town Quay and Royal Pier Tramway
Chapel Tramway
Bull's Run Tramway
Northam Wharves Tramway